HOW TO GET A FREE BOOB JOB

and other insights from a breast cancer adventurer

Penny Casselman

BALBOA.PRESS
A DIVISION OF HAY HOUSE

Copyright © 2020 Penny Casselman.

All rights reserved. No part of this book may be used or reproduced by any means, graphic, electronic, or mechanical, including photocopying, recording, taping or by any information storage retrieval system without the written permission of the author except in the case of brief quotations embodied in critical articles and reviews.

Balboa Press books may be ordered through booksellers or by contacting:

Balboa Press
A Division of Hay House
1663 Liberty Drive
Bloomington, IN 47403
www.balboapress.com
844-682-1282

Because of the dynamic nature of the Internet, any web addresses or links contained in this book may have changed since publication and may no longer be valid. The views expressed in this work are solely those of the author and do not necessarily reflect the views of the publisher, and the publisher hereby disclaims any responsibility for them.

The author of this book does not dispense medical advice or prescribe the use of any technique as a form of treatment for physical, emotional, or medical problems without the advice of a physician, either directly or indirectly. The intent of the author is only to offer information of a general nature to help you in your quest for emotional and spiritual well-being. In the event you use any of the information in this book for yourself, which is your constitutional right, the author and the publisher assume no responsibility for your actions.

Any people depicted in stock imagery provided by Getty Images are models, and such images are being used for illustrative purposes only. Certain stock imagery © Getty Images.

Print information available on the last page.

ISBN: 978-1-9822-5471-1 (sc)
ISBN: 978-1-9822-5473-5 (hc)
ISBN: 978-1-9822-5472-8 (e)

Library of Congress Control Number: 2020917256

Balboa Press rev. date: 10/21/2020

"Tell the story of the mountain you climbed. Your words could be a page in someone else's survival guide."

~ *Morgan Harper Nichols*

Contents

Acknowledgments...xiii
Introduction...xv

PART ONE
The "C" Word and First Steps

A Younger Me..2
The Letter...5
So This is Happening..10
Biopsy Day..13
Time for a Pep Talk..14
Wonder Woman..15
Coming Full Circle..18
'Twas the Night before Surgery 24
Post Surgery Update..27
The Day After...28
Wednesday Morning Update..32
Happy Dance!..35

PART TWO
Prep, Prep, Prep for All To Come

The Carousel of Change..40
Drum Roll, Please!..41

Cry Me a River 45
I'm in the Club! 50
Happy Boobsday, I Mean Tuesday! 54
Where Does the Time Go? 57
Echo, Drain, and Port 59
Got My Wig(s) ON! 62
Oh YES. I. DID. 65

PART THREE
Chemo

A Solid Routine 70
Snow White, Sleepy 71
One Down, Eleven to Go 75
3/16" is SHORT 78
Three Minute Miracle 83
Groundhog Day 84
Flattery Will Get You Far! 86
Twelve Hours 91
Pensive 94
Mini Milestone Monday 99
Second and Ten 100
Hot Mess, By the Numbers 105
Game ON! 107

PART FOUR
Now for My Next Phase

Our Unique Paths 110
Wait! Was Yesterday Monday?! 111
The Countdown Begins 117
Phase Two 119
And, They're Off! 123
Back to Reality 126

Dear Santa...132
Congratulations!..135

PART FIVE
Surgery Round One

Live in the Moment..138
I, Penny...140
Surgery Day Update...145
I Live!..146
Home..147
Five Days Out...149
Wild, Wild West..157
Chasing ZZZ's Like a Champ..160
Can You Hear Me Now?..164
The More You Know..166
DUH!..170
Now What?..176
0.804...180
Blarney, Blooms, and Boulders..182
Here We Grow Again...184

PART SIX
Boob Job!

My Superheroes..188
Well, Hello There!...191
Tomorrow Dawns a New Day!..195
Tomorrow Has Arrived..199
Surgery Update...200
Home...201
Go Go Gadget...203
Just Hanging Around...208
Strap In and Hold On..210
Twelve and Holding...216

PART SEVEN
What's Next?

A Good Challenge	220
Countdowns Galore!	222
Fireworks, Baby!	224
The End of an Era	227
It's Official	234
The Letter S	238
This is Life	242
Flashback	244
Conclusion	249
Chronology of Events	253

For my mom.

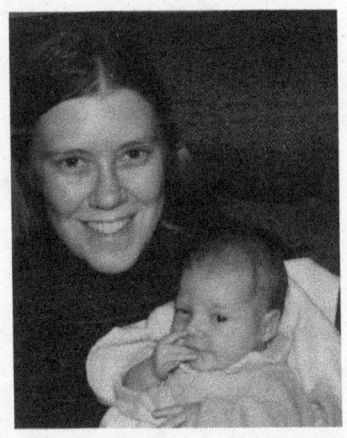

Gloria Jeanne Casselman (nee Mielke)
December 8, 1947–September 18, 1980

Acknowledgments

Days after receiving my cancer diagnosis, the CaringBridge updates began to flow. I wrote them out of necessity, but everyone around me saw it differently—I was becoming an author. Now, at the conclusion of my memoir, I've got armfuls of gratitude to bestow and a lot of people to thank. Ready? Let's go.

To you, a member of my medical team at MetroHealth. Your smiles gave me hope, your care was palpable, and your concern for my comfort eased my fears. When I faced challenging times, you were the reason I could get up and drag myself to appointments, infusions, procedures, and surgeries. Your fierce advocacy for my health is the reason I am here today. A bonus I never saw coming? Your friendship. Priceless. I (heart) you; now and always.

To you, my Casselman or Mielke immediate family member or relative. You endured watching my mom fight, and ultimately lose, her battle against breast cancer forty years ago. I cannot begin to understand the rollercoaster of emotions you experienced upon hearing the news of my diagnosis. Yet, you rallied behind me, and I stand in awe. I was the canary in the coal mine, and we both had to come to grips with a disease passed down from one generation to another. This was not only my adventure but a piece of yours as well. You are brave, beyond measure, and I love you more than you will ever know.

To you, my adopted family and Gabrosek clan member. Your support, smiles, laughs, hugs, and encouragement kept my spirits high, and that's exactly what I needed during this adventure. Thank you, from the bottom of my heart.

For you, my friend. You called me, texted me, mailed me a card, sent me flowers, brought me food, surprised me with gifts, made me laugh, checked in on me at home, visited me in the hospital, gave me gentle hugs, listened when I cried, and never stopped sending me good vibes. Know that you made my days brighter and helped to shorten my recovery time. You are a part of the family I choose, and I love you to the moon and back.

To you, my Kickstarter supporter. You believed in me, in my vision, and put hard cash down to make this book a reality. I hope I didn't disappoint, fingers crossed. Without you, the ink on this page may never have been printed. A special callout to the following top tier supporters: Norm and Martha, Mayda and Ted, Ann and Joe, Joe, Jessie and Sean, Bridgette and Steve, Tony, and Colleen. Know that when safe times return, we'll gather in person to celebrate! That's a promise you can take to the bank!

For you, my connection from the Gathering Place. Your understanding, insights, and kindness made traversing this adventure a little less lonely. I will cherish your friendship, always.

Last, but certainly not least, my editor Dayna. Without your keen eye for detail, attention to narrative, and understanding of the story I wanted to share, this book would not be the gem I am so proud of today. I'm so grateful the universe found a way for our paths to cross, thank you.

Introduction

The month of May had arrived, and the occasion of my birth was about to begin its annual month-long celebration. For the record, it's officially the seventh. This year, 2017, marked number forty-five. Parties were planned, happy hours scheduled, and family celebrations were all marked on the calendar. During this month, no reasonable celebratory request was turned down. In between all the festivities, however, mundane tasks still demanded moments of my time—things like voting for a local tax initiative, an air conditioning tune-up, gutter cleaning, and a mammogram. That last activity, although easy, routine, and necessary, would be the catalyst that would reshape my life and set me on a trajectory I thought I had escaped.

Throughout this adventure, I've learned many things about myself and others, too, for that matter, just one of which is that I can write. I'm comfortable with my voice and sharing, and I realized that not only is writing helpful for me but it also casts light on my situation for others to understand, absorb, and experience the journey along with me. I also want to recognize I'm not imparting any insight that, perhaps, hasn't already been delivered by someone else at another time in another book. What I am an expert at is sharing my experience in my voice, at my own pace, with my unique life filters through which I write my story.

This book contains many entries from CaringBridge; the first entry is from 2017. CaringBridge.org is an online platform like Facebook but designed to support individuals facing a health crisis. Throughout this book, you'll find I dart between two realities. My CaringBridge entries—set apart with dates, titles, large margins, and a center page position—are raw, sometimes graphic, often amusing, occasionally sad, and frequently pensive. Each one offers a glimpse of me in real-time facing my unknown future. In 2016, I watched a close friend navigate her BRCA1 diagnosis and, sadly, succumb to it after a five-year battle. I often felt numb because I couldn't wrap my head around what she was enduring. I realize each cancer journey is unique. And that even if we both happen to arrive at the same destination, our paths look different. However, I hope these CaringBridge sections give you insight as to what the journey felt like for me in the moment. I feel that these are important snapshots of what I was going through and what, I believe, many in my position grapple with along the way. For that reason, I have not drastically altered these—aside from correcting an occasional misspelling, formatting issue, or adding meaningful details to ensure clarity for you, the reader.

I have also included the "me of today"—sounds like a ride at Disney World, no? "Today's me" offers my reflections and a new narrative presented to you like the words you're reading now—taking full advantage of the page width and smaller margins. This voice is the me that has had years to ponder, reflect, embrace, and grow through every test, diagnosis, surgery, doctor visit, infusion, and procedure into the person I am today.

Quick caveat, I'm not a doctor. Although I offer some descriptions of medical procedures and explanations of my treatment options, they are just that, my options and my choices. So, as you join me on this adventure, please know my words are not advice—medical or otherwise—for you or anyone you may know dealing with a similar situation. Think of them as potential starting points for questions to ask a trusted medical professional about the best options for you.

Regardless of your affiliation with cancer, after reading this book, I hope you walk away with a few nuggets of insight, sparks of inspiration, and new perspectives to lean on when facing the wild unknown. Change is a constant in life—and learning to befriend it makes navigating life so much more enjoyable. But above all, I hope that this book shows those of you who are facing a similar journey, either yourself or thorough a loved one, that you are not alone.

Without further ado, let's dive in.

PART ONE

The "C" Word and First Steps

A Younger Me

When I was a kid, I'd get tonsillitis quite frequently. And for the record, I still have my tonsils, amazingly. I recall one bout when I was running a fever—I knew it was bad because I didn't even have enough energy to play. I lay lifeless under an afghan my grandma had made, curled up on our cream, tan, and black zigzag patterned sofa. The cushions that cuddled me were the same cushions that acted as walls when we built forts in the living room and also cushioned our landings as we launched ourselves into aerial front flips off the arms of the sofa. *Whee!* My dad came to check on me and took a seat next to me to check my temperature; he administered some medicine and asked how I was feeling. I remember looking into his eyes—my own starting to well up—and asking him if I was going to die. I must have been eight at the time—my mom's funeral fresh in my memory, and her now notable absence from my side nursing me back to health fueled my concerned question. I don't recall his exact words, but I remember the look of sadness on his face. I'm sure the look carried with it a million emotions he must have been feeling. Heartbroken that his eight-year-old daughter was asking about the possibility of her death. Somber in the realization that this was not the life he had ever imagined having—raising two young children alone. Wistful for days past when everyone was happy and healthy. His look lasted only a moment before he held my hand and assured me I wasn't going to die and that soon enough I would be feeling better, I just had to rest.

During my adolescence, the question of my possible death surfaced several times—usually spawned by a stuffy nose, fever, and a few hacking coughs. Luckily, for my dad's sanity and mine, too, maturity brought forth the understanding of cancer. That combined with the assurance from doctors that my mom's death was an anomaly and not a fate I was eminently facing, the death questions stopped—verbally, anyway. As I entered my teens, the questions started again, this time only in my mind and only on my birthday. At first, they were just faint whispers and would dart in and out as quickly as a hummingbird. It wasn't until my mid-twenties when the whispers became soft knocks, like a visitor who doesn't want the door to open, they just wanted to say they had tried to stop by and see you and are so sorry they missed you—all the while you sat ten feet from the front door oblivious to the faint knocks. The questions made their last thundering appearance on the occasion of my thirty-third birthday. That was the year I had officially lived longer on this earth than my mom.

To say that birthday was sobering is an understatement. I felt young. I was newly married. I didn't have kids. The thought of my mom fighting cancer for five years blew my mind. It hit me how short her life was. Part of me was sad all over again that she died. A part of me felt awkward that I was still living. And part of me breathed a sigh of relief that I had lived past my mom. I was out of the woods. When I turned forty, I let the thought of cancer go. I was sure that by making it eight years beyond my mom that I had crushed the odds and was free and clear to live the rest of my life without the looming fear of cancer. That wasn't my future.

Over the years, the gaps would lengthen between thinking of my mom's death. First, just a few days would pass, then weeks, and now I feel guilty sometimes that I don't think of her for months—that she was a blip in my history. My mom was a talented and focused woman. She was musically gifted and played both the trumpet and piano. She was a majorette. And just a few short weeks after my first birthday, she walked across the stage to receive her master's in education. I often wonder what I would be like today if she had lived to raise me to adulthood? Would I have had more success in my corporate life? Would I have been valedictorian of my high school class? As it is, I was way off the mark for either one of those outcomes. Having the benefit of hindsight, I wouldn't want my life to be any different. That may sound harsh—and after reading it over again, I might agree. But honestly, I like the woman I am today, and I don't think I'd be here under any other circumstances.

The Letter

Friday, May 26, 2017

    I received a letter informing me I'd need to have an ultrasound on my right breast because "Your recent mammogram showed a finding that requires additional imaging for a complete evaluation." I called and scheduled the follow-up ultrasound for the morning of June 1.

    To be fair, I'm not too worried at this point. I've had this request made in the past because I have dense breast tissue, gone through the motions, and everything was ok.

    Penny "Been There, Done That" Casselman

I had scheduled my ultrasound as a quick stop on my way out of town. A four-hour drive that day separated me and a four-day music festival outside of Athens, Ohio. The medical center that conducted the ultrasounds wasn't too far out of my way and—since I had this request made of me before with no adverse outcome—I figured I'd just knock it out before a long weekend of music, sweltering heat, and fun with friends.

Every Step of the Way

Thursday, June 1, 2017

I went in for my ultrasound. After the technician snapped several images of my breast, she said she would show them to the radiologist on duty and that, if they felt it was needed, the radiologist may come in to conduct a second ultrasound for themselves. Ok, cool. UNTIL the radiologist came in, started to do her exam, and said: "Blah, blah, blah . . . we'll be with you every step of the way." WAIT! WHAT?! Turn on the waterworks. She explained a bit about why there was increased concern and that I would need a biopsy, but first I'd need to speak with a surgeon.

I may have gotten some details wrong here. Thinking back, I *only* remember four things:

1. The radiologist saying, "We'll be with you every step of the way."
2. Her comment about the edges of the mass being fuzzy in the images.
3. The radiologist giving me a hug after asking me, "What are your initial concerns?" I told

her my mom died when I was eight of cancer, starting in the breast.
4. The news that the mass was less than one centimeter in diameter.

This day was rough!
Penny "Clęarly NOT out of the Woods" Casselman

Honestly, rough was an understatement. Those nine words uttered by the radiologist are seared into my brain like no others. I needed to leave stat. I quickly got dressed, wiped away the tears that had streamed down my cheeks, and took a few deep breaths. I could hardly get words out when I emerged to grab Joe, my boyfriend, from the waiting area so we could exit the complex. His look of concern made everything I was experiencing worse, although it wasn't his fault. When I pulled him down the hall, my eyes were already red and swollen and my tears had taken most of my mascara off.

I gave him the keys to the car and said he had the wheel now. I buckled myself in and sat in stunned silence. We made our way to the freeway, and as he drove, my eyes just stared blankly out the passenger window, watching the world whiz by. I could tell Joe wanted to comfort me, that he wanted to reassure me it was going to be ok, but I'm glad he kept quiet. Although my gaze was empty, my mind was racing. Every thought of what if, maybe, why me, why now, did this just really happen, I don't want to die, I want to live, I want to fight, I just wanna scream were all clamoring atop each other for attention. I knew if I had to answer a question or respond to a comment, the floodgates would open again. I'm sure it was difficult for Joe to stay silent, but I appreciated his restraint. I needed a reprieve and some silence. The weight in the car was heavy, and I was worried that one more tear or word or glance would suddenly have the tail pipe dragging—figuratively, of course. Just two hours before, I was elated the sun was shining and that it was expected to do so the entire balance of the weekend. Now, all I wanted to see was gray clouds; how dare mother nature smile and exude happiness after this news. Dammit, I wanted torrential rain, bitter cold, and blustery winds; all things that demand you get under the covers, curl up in a ball, and just sleep—immune to the world and alone.

I have no idea how many miles passed before I spoke. My first audible thought: I don't want any of our housemates to know about what just occurred. I knew my weekend would be mired in sadness with thoughts of mortality and uncertainty as to what lay ahead of me. I certainly didn't want to be the dark cloud over anyone else's fun-filled weekend; I'd reserve that for myself, thank you very much.

The festival was flamin' hot. Not the acts per se, although they were decent that year, but the weather. It was almost unbearable for a Casper like me. Each morning, I'd lather up with sunscreen, don a hat, hide behind sunnies, and slip into the lightest pieces of clothing I had packed. Once seated in my folding portable camping chair at the main stage, I remained motionless; even turning my head was too much effort and could cause me to break out into a feverish sweat. Did I mention there was no shade to be found? I suppose I should be thankful it was so hot; I honestly couldn't focus on anything other than listening to the music and not moving. My pending medical diagnosis was a distant third for priorities, and for that, I was thankful.

Joe did his best over the weekend to ease my mind, saying we needed to wait for the biopsy and subsequent results as the ultrasound, after all, wasn't a concrete diagnosis. I wished I could have shared in his frail optimism. Even though no biopsy had yet been performed, I knew I had cancer. Why? I reasoned with myself that the radiologist reviews ultrasounds All. Day. Long. It's their job, their specialty, their expertise. During high school, I worked for a summer at the local grocery store, assigned to the deli department. Within a few weeks, I could grab a handful of cold cuts, plop them on the digital scale, and get it within one-tenth of a pound, with my eyes closed. If I could master grabbing a nearly perfect pound of meat in my hand, surely a trained radiologist could identify cancer by sight with a high degree of certainty.

Wanting to keep this process moving along at warp speed, I had asked the hospital to call me on Friday—at the festival—so I could schedule my initial consultation with a surgeon. Regardless of biopsy outcome, I would need surgery to remove the mass. I waited for a break between sets to slip away from my chair. I wanted to find somewhere relatively quiet, and preferably in the shade, from which to return the call from the hospital. The break came, I found shade, and the scheduler and I settled on June 6, just two days after getting home, to speak with the surgeon.

So This is Happening

Tuesday, June 6, 2017

This was my first meeting with my surgeon, Dr. Hauer. He did a manual exam to feel the mass and a cursory scan of my lymph nodes. Side note here, his manual exam of my lymph nodes did not detect any masses. Before determining the exact nature of the surgery, he indicated I'd need a biopsy of the breast mass tissue. Not wasting any time, which I thoroughly appreciated, his office was able to secure a June 7th morning appointment for my biopsy procedure. In addition, we also scheduled two other appointments: The first was my follow-up visit for Tuesday, June 13, during which time I'd most likely be getting the results and discussing surgery options with Dr. Hauer. The second was an appointment on Thursday, June 15, with a genetic counselor to conduct genetic testing for known abnormal functioning genes strongly related to cancers of this nature. I like Dr. Hauer. He's very personable and has an excellent bedside manner; his nurse practitioner (Anna) is pretty swell too.

How To Get A Free Boob Job

Penny "Strap In. The Ride Is About to Begin" Casselman

I've always been a doer; for this, I can thank my dad. Ever since I can remember, honestly, I'd follow him around and assist with every home improvement project I could. There's a photo of me that I love, taken when I was about three, when I was helping my dad paint the wall a cool shade of mint.

Three-year-old Penny learning to hold a brush and paint with her dad.

Over the years, there was always a long list of home improvement projects to accomplish. When one had been completed, it was on to the next. Even though some projects tested me both physically and mentally, I knew what was waiting for me at the end—a massive sense of pride and awe in what I had accomplished. Along the way, I had solved problems, learned new skills, got creative, and, as a result, I was left with something more impressive than what I started with. Receiving an abrupt medical diagnosis was just another project for me to tackle. There would be numerous tasks to test me mentally and physically, and they would require me to learn new skills. Unlike all the projects I had assisted my dad with, drawing on his vast experience and knowledge to help maneuver whatever setback we might encounter, this one would be a mostly solo endeavor. I had to believe that what was waiting for me on the other side would indeed be worth my effort—just like all the other projects that had come before me.

Biopsy Day

Wednesday, June 7, 2017

This was a quick, quite painless, and easy procedure. Honestly, having a mole removed is more painful than what was performed, in my humble opinion. Now the awful waiting begins.

Penny "That Wasn't So Bad" Casselman

Patience, although a noble virtue, isn't one of my strongest suits. I'm a "let's keep this bus movin'" kinda gal. I like progress. I like results. I don't labor over decisions ad nauseam, as that can send me down rabbit holes far too deep, dark, and unproductive for my temperament. Progress is more important than perfection, right? Well, maybe.

Time for a Pep Talk

Wednesday, June 7, 2017

Nearly every moment of every day, I keep telling myself, "You have cancer, but it's no big deal, they're catching it early. This isn't the 1970s, when Mom was diagnosed, and medical treatments have come a long way. I'm going to stay strong, ask lots of questions of the doctor, and map out a plan to evict this mass! End. Of. Story."

Penny "No Worries. I Got This!" Casselman

Wonder Woman

Tuesday, June 13, 2017

Ok, hearing that you have cancer from a medical professional, in a white coat, in a hospital exam room, while sitting on an exam table is NOT the same as telling yourself. Sigh. I stayed strong, focused, and eyes dry until I rounded the final twenty minutes of the appointment, when the waterworks started again. I was proud of myself as I kept my breathing in check, maintained a calm demeanor, and joked that the facial tissue—which was the size of a square of toilet paper—was a little scratchy and slightly subpar for an environment of this type. *Ha!*

We discussed options and settled on surgery as soon as possible, Friday, June 23. My surgery will be a lumpectomy and a removal of the sentinel lymph node near my right breast. This procedure is outpatient, so I'll be home in familiar surroundings by late afternoon, yay!

Here's where the doer side of me kicked into high gear. I began my feverish pitch of appointment scheduling. After all, my life was turning into one grand project filled with task after task after task. Let's get to the end, shall we? Little did I fully realize how long this project was going to take—certainly longer than it takes to paint a dining room, or any room for that matter, a pale shade of mint. Although Dr. Hauer and I planned a quick turnaround for surgery, I found myself slightly bummed, as I would have to wait weeks for the results of my genetic testing. I had the option to postpone surgery until after my genetic test results were returned, which could potentially save me an additional surgery. Still, neither of us had any idea how fast my cancer was growing. The mass hadn't seemed to have spread yet, but what if it was going to spread tomorrow, or in those days between now and when the results came in? All immediate signs pointed to a singular one-site mass. If it did spread before surgery, I would always have wondered if I could have stopped it by being more aggressive with my decision; those thoughts were too heavy for this gal to think about forever. And so, my first surgery would proceed ASAP, with genetics to follow.

This is a lot to digest, I know. Here are a few other FAQs you might be wondering about.

Q: What stage is your cancer?
A: I won't know this information until the biopsy of my sentinel lymph node is complete. I've been told the biopsy results usually take three weeks, so right now, I'm looking at mid-July for before I can provide further clarity.

Q: How big is the cancer mass?
A: Good news, the silver lining here, is the mass is less than one centimeter in diameter. My entire team of medical professionals agree that this is an early catch. Yay!

Q: Will you need radiation or chemotherapy?

A: All signs point to *yes*, for both. Honestly, not the news I wanted to hear, but I'd rather go through this now and never have to deal with it again! You see, given my young age of forty-five (yes, I'm still a youngster!), they want to be aggressive with my treatments, ensuring they've eradicated any and every cancer cell in my body. Bam! Especially, you know, given that I'm a youngster in good health, my body can more efficiently bounce back from treatments. No one is keeping this Wonder Woman down!

Well, friend, that's all for now. Certainly more updates to come, so stay tuned.

With much *love* and *gratitude*!

xoxo

Penny "Where's My Cape?" Casselman

Coming Full Circle

Saturday, June 17, 2017

Quick Penny fact: I wanted to be a genetic counselor when I entered college.

I find it crazy that now I find myself consulting one to get the details on my genetic lineage.

So, you might be thinking, "Gosh Penny, you sure did land pretty far away from that profession." Yes. I. Did. Here's why:

1. Me and chemistry, not such good friends. We tried to work it out, really, and finally parted ways with huge mutual respect.
2. I figured I had enough problems of my own that I didn't need to participate in a profession where I would deliver sad news to others on a routine basis. To be fair, they also provide good news sometimes.

Ok, enough about my undergraduate pursuits.

Thursday morning was my initial appointment with Elizabeth Hogan, my genetic counselor. Again, I cannot say enough good things about *everyone* at MetroHealth; the people there are amazingly kind, caring, and professional.

The office of genetic testing wasn't located in the most expected of locations; it was nestled in the far corner of the pediatrics ward. Taking a deep breath, I opened the door and crossed the threshold into the land of munchkins; they were everywhere. The waiting room smelled of hand sanitizer, diapers, and fruit snacks. Perhaps a new Glade scent opportunity? *Ha!* I checked in and then turned to find a seat while I waited, there was nowhere for me to sit to escape the running, screaming, laughing, crying, sneezing, coughing, gaming, arguing little ones—nowhere. I beelined for the few seats close to the door where I would be taken back to meet with Elizabeth.

Finally, after what seemed like hours—it was ten minutes—Elizabeth appeared and called me back. The path back to her office had us passing dozens of pediatric exam rooms. The mood back there was slightly tempered since now the munchkins couldn't run free but instead were confined to the four walls of their exam room—thankfully I didn't have to worry about tripping or stepping on any of them.

Elizabeth's office reminded me of my undergraduate dorm room. Small, stark, and devoid of personality—utilitarian. Quick caveat, in the latter part of my corporate career, that's how I treated my offices, especially after I was downsized for the third time. I told myself I never wanted to have more than a single box of personal effects to pack up, as I fully expected to be the victim of another corporate downsizing before I retired. You can see, then, how I appreciated her streamlined environment. I sat down in one of the two industrial stackable chairs, Elizabeth and I exchanged pleasantries, and then the deep dive conversation began.

We chatted about my family tree: who's had cancer, who hasn't, how old they were, what type, blah blah blah. Honestly, I didn't realize how many people in my family have had some form of cancer; strange how quickly it exits your mind once they are back to being healthy again, or dead. Whoa! I'm not morbid or pessimistic here, nor do I think I have one foot in the grave, quite the opposite (remember Wonder Woman?)! It's just the living, well, keep on living, and your own life, again, takes center stage. You get it, I hope.

Elizabeth talked about the genetic tests that would be conducted with the sample of blood I was to donate thirty minutes later. I'm having a panel of thirty-four genes checked, with a group of six requested to have their results expedited. The entire group of thirty-four looks at genes known for their contribution to various forms of cancer, while the subset of six is directly linked to breast/cervical/uterine/ovarian cancer; ya' know, the girlie kind of genes. A caveat, genetic testing is relatively new, and therefore my mom's doctors didn't have access to such knowledge or insights in the '70s.

As I mentioned in my last update, I'm not expecting to receive the results of these genetic tests until early July. "But wait a minute! I thought six are being expedited?" Ah, yes, you are correct! Here's the thing, even though they are being expedited, I still won't have the results until *after* my surgery occurs.

In the interest of time, I wanted to move swiftly to evict the unwanted mass (you see it's not paying rent, very annoying) and, therefore, made the decision *not* to wait for the return of the genetic results.

At this point, you might be asking yourself, "Wait, what? Why wouldn't you wait for the results? This all seems out of order, no?" Rest assured, I'll cover in detail my, and my doctor's, reasoning to proceed when (spoiler alert!) I reveal the testing results. I won't leave you hanging, pinky swear.

So, what does this all mean? (Have I mentioned you ask such good questions?)
I'm having surgery this coming Friday, June 23, to address the mass already identified and get it out! Depending on the outcome of the genetic tests, the biopsy of the mass with surrounding tissue, and the biopsy of the sentinel lymph node, I *may* be looking at additional surgeries; more about all that as results roll in.
Waiting for the various results will seem like the longest wait of my life; distractions will be welcome! (Hint, hint.)

I wanted as much on my calendar as possible. I wanted every minute of every day filled to the brim so I couldn't think of anything else except "Who am I seeing next?" and "What are we doing?" Crickets. Hmmm. I started to reflect on why the offers weren't rolling in, and it hit me: no one knew what to do. I found it uncomfortable being super specific with my initial ask. Asking for help—in this scenario, inviting others to fill my calendar with events—was a slight admission that I was operating at less than optimal levels. A stark realization that things in my world weren't, well, normal. I realized I needed to be direct, so all my future requests would come with actionable items to select from. The most straightforward request—and one that most people I guessed could rally around—was dinner drop-offs on the days I would receive chemo. I knew the last thing I'd want to do after spending nearly all day at the hospital was to come home wondering what I wanted for dinner. It worked like a charm and each time I had food for days! Best. Decision. Ever.

Lastly, have you heard of this thing called retail therapy? I've recently done some research and found that it is, indeed, very therapeutic and good for both your outer and inner energy! I've attached a picture of just one of my latest acquisitions, this FAB statement necklace. I wore it to meet with my surgeon and, again, when meeting with my genetic counselor. Do you think they'll let me wear it into the OR?

I now own fifteen statement necklaces. I love them all but rarely wear them—I need to rectify that, but I digress. During my weeks and months of infusions, tests, and procedures, however, they brought me happiness, a sense of normalcy, and exuded tons of sparkle when my own was lacking.

Remember, it's better to look good than to feel good!

(Ok, yes yes yes, I'd rather be healthy; but looking good is a close second!)

With love, gratitude, and grace until my next entry.

Penny "Does This Necklace Make My Boobs Look Big?" Casselman

'Twas the Night before Surgery . . .

Thursday, June 22, 2017

. . . and all through the house, the shoe decision was lingering, which pair to bounce?

It's true. Only Penny, right?

In keeping with my retail therapy regime, I picked up some strappy, gold, sparkly pumps; *I love them*! I *so* want to wear them to the surgery center tomorrow morning. After careful thought, I finally realized that walking *into* the surgery center would not be an issue, walking *out*, however, might prove extremely difficult—you know, all hopped up on anesthesia. Therefore, in being a responsible adult, I'll be wearing my more sensible flat oxfords.

A quick note before tomorrow. Here's the scoop on timing and what you, my eager reader, can expect:

1. I will arrive at the surgery center at 7:45 a.m.
2. I'll get prepped and ready for my scheduled surgery time at 9:00 a.m.

3. Anticipating that everything will go just fine, I should be wheeled out of the OR around eleven a.m. as this is usually a two-hour surgery.
4. Still drooling on myself, ha, I'll lay on the gurney until enough anesthesia has exited my body and allowed my eyes to open and my mouth to utter some, what I'm sure will be, profound thoughts like "I need some water" or "Can I have a cracker?"
5. Before I'm released to go home, Joe will provide a journal update so you'll know my status; please be patient.

Some additional notes on my surgery. The nitty-gritty details.

Once I'm under and dreaming of high heels and lipstick, they'll remove, as is planned right now, the mass in my breast and my right sentinel lymph node. Since I've already had a biopsy on my mass, the surgeon already knows it's cancerous. What's unknown, until surgery time, is if the cancer has spread to the lymph nodes. I won't be out of the woods yet, my follow-up appointment with Dr. Hauer is at 9:00 a.m. on June 30 where he'll check the progress of my healing, discuss the pathology reports on the lymph node, and, fingers crossed, I'll also receive the genetic results from the expedited panel of six genes. All of these results will help to establish the protocol for the next steps in my cancer adventure.

I plan to provide another journal update once I've rested for a day or so and can be assured that my mind can string together several coherent thoughts and that my fingers can execute the typing.

All good vibes, prayers, mojo, and the like are being accepted at this time; I don't discriminate.

With love, gratitude, and kisses to you.

Penny "Visions of Sugar Plums" Casselman

Post Surgery Update

Friday, June 23, 2017

Hi friends and family, Joe here.

Penny's surgeon, Dr. Hauer, just visited me in the waiting room and gave me a thumbs up. The surgery went well, Penny did great, and she is in post-op and resting comfortably.

There are many details to share, I'll leave that to Penny, but here are a few:

- The medical staff here took great care of Penny—and me too.

- While surgery prep wasn't much fun, when I left Penny she was in good spirits and ready to go.

- Unfortunately, Penny didn't wear her fab new high heels, the weather just didn't cooperate.

Thanks for your thoughts and prayers, and more news to come soon.

Joe

The Day After

Saturday, June 24, 2017

I'm up, moving about, and showered, no longer stinky and orange from the surgical prep!

I don't know what they did when they intubated me, but my throat is *sore* and red. I'm still a bit tired. My armpit is sore and so is my breast, although, to be honest, I think my throat hurts the most. Thanks for your patience with my update, here we go!

First thing first, I wore my sparkly, flat oxford shoes. I know, I know, I know, I so wanted to be fabulous walking into the surgery center in my heels; however, the torrential downpour that morning was sure to ruin them, and I can't have that!

This is the kind of weather I wanted to have on the day I had my ultrasound. Gray skies, foggy, and rain. It was the perfect weather for surgery since I wasn't going to feel guilty about being inside the entire day, in June, in Cleveland.

I arrived on time, and they got straight to business; for the record, I had no idea how much prep was involved for my surgery! First, I donned a standard-issue hospital gown and matching grippy socks. I then met the intake nurse who recorded my vitals and immediately whisked me up to Nuclear Medicine, where I received four shots, each containing a small dose of radioactivity, in four different areas in my right breast. Good times. THEN I had to massage my breast to help the uptake of the radioactivity to my lymph nodes; we're off to a great and fun start. Did I mention I wasn't given a numbing agent before the injections?

Next, I got wheeled up to the breast imaging center, where they placed a wire into the mass to create a road map for the surgeon. This ensured he could easily identify and fully extract it during surgery. Side note, said wire stuck out of my breast about three inches; oh, my! Immediately after getting "wiretapped," I had three different mammogram images taken to ensure the placement of the wire was satisfactory. Yep, on top of everything thus far, they smashed my breast into a pancake, three times.

Finally, I was taken down to my final waiting area, just outside where my surgery would take place. *Yay!* I got my IV for fluids, antibiotics, and for the administration of the happy juice soon to follow. As if this wasn't enough, the nurse then said I required one more shot, a single dose of blood thinner. I got to choose between my arm and my belly—*what*?! I opted for the arm.

Fortunately, this would clock in as the fifth surgery of my life. Although, this was, by far, the most serious. I knew from experience that you don't just waltz into a hospital, sign your name, and get whisked back to the operating room. Having vitals taken and chatting with your surgeon, the supporting nurses, and the anesthesiologist were all standard fare. This surgery, however, had many more moving parts than I was expecting. I'm glad I wasn't given a full roadmap of events since I would have become overwhelmed, especially with the anticipation of every needle poke and breast image required to ensure a successful outcome. In this instance, for sure, ignorance was bliss.

>Happy juice was administered, and I was dreaming of lipstick and heels.
>I came through with flying colors; Dr. Hauer gave me a thumbs up.
>He removed the mass without incident and felt good about the margins (i.e., he felt he had grabbed enough of the surrounding tissue to have captured all of the cancer cells). Of course, pathology still needs to review the tissue in detail before a final sign-off that all is clear.
>About the lymph nodes: they took five.

That was way more than I was expecting! A single node—as the sentinel name would suggest—was the number I expected to be removed. Apparently, the surrounding nodes were jealous and wanted in on the action too—they certainly didn't want to get left behind and miss all the fun! You might be asking, what the what?

>Here's how I can explain it. If you're an only child, your parents can easily say who's their favorite; you are! If, however, you have siblings, it becomes a much more difficult, almost impossible, question to answer; they love you all the same! So goes my lymph nodes, sibling-like. You see, there

was a cluster so near each other that they couldn't pick just *one* to call the sentinel, so they opted to treat them all equally and out they came. Since no others were taken, I see that as a good sign. Just like the mass, additional review by pathology is necessary for a definitive result.

What next? I wait.

My follow-up appointment with Dr. Hauer is Friday, June 30. I'll get the results from the removed mass and lymph nodes and should also have the results from the expedited panel of six genes from the genetic screening. There will be *lots* to discuss, and we'll have to plan the next steps, many of which depend upon the results of all the tests combined.

I cannot thank you enough for your kind words, loving gestures, and positive energy. This certainly wasn't anything I had ever planned to deal with, and I have massive evidence that my family and the family I choose (my friends) are second to none! You keep me smiling and focused on many, many, many more bright and happy times ahead.

Until my next post.

xoxo

. Penny "My Dad's Favorite Daughter" Casselman

Wednesday Morning Update

Wednesday, June 28, 2017

    Forty-eight hours to go.

My post-op follow-up appointment is this Friday, June 30, at 9:00 a.m. I'm keeping all appendages crossed that the results of the lymph node biopsy, the clear margins on the mass, and my expedited panel of six genes for genetic testing will be available for review and discussion. I'm a planner, and it's crippling that my calendar is seemingly void of events. While it makes me sad, since I don't know what lies ahead, I'm keeping it empty, for now. Yes, I *could* schedule things, but I hate to cancel, so I deal with a blank calendar. I am keeping things in perspective (i.e., I'm not jumping to conclusions as to what the test results will reveal, as that would be completely counterproductive).

    This past weekend I was delighted to host my dad and brother. They made the trip here to rally for me, and it was *wonderful*! We went to brunch, cooked out on the grill, and saw the Alex Katz exhibit at the Cleveland Museum of Art. You're probably thinking to yourself, "*Holy cow*, you did all that just days after surgery?" Yes. I. Did. With one caveat, I had *lots* of naps and took advantage of the extra hands on deck to get some to-dos checked off my list; I'm a good supervisor!

I'm able to take showers, drive, eat whatever I want, so I look and act pretty normal. Aside from my usual two daily naps(yes, hobbits get two breakfasts, I get two naps), I'm feeling pretty good! All of this is slightly difficult to process. Everyone is concerned about me, but I don't look "sick." I know I can't lift heavy things with my right side, as I can feel the underlying strain to my incision site and then immediately cease to attempt the activity. Allow me to clarify one thing: I look well when clothed. Underneath those clothes however, my right breast and underarm looked like they went on a bender in Vegas and participated in several bar fights—you should have seen the other guy.

What else is difficult to process is this, I'm still a *long* way off, relatively speaking, from being done with this adventure. Depending upon the various combinations of results I'll get on Friday, I'm looking at the potential for more surgery and a high chance of radiation and chemo. Not the most uplifting forecast. I know, I know, this is *all* necessary so that I live a long, happy, and healthy life, cancer free! I mean, who else is going to give you fashion and decorating advice in your retirement?!

Keep sending your positive energy my way; it's always welcomed; I *know* it's working!

Much love to you.

xo

Penny "I'm in it for the long haul" Casselman

Up to this point, my cancer adventure had been a more mental challenge rather than a physical one. This surgery, however, was a glimpse into what the next year would look like. Now there were visual reminders of what I was going through in the form of bruises, newly acquired scars, and the beginning of deformity to the body I was born into. To be fair, my body wasn't perfect before all this started. My boobs weren't the same size, and one was slightly vertically challenged. Thank goodness for the technical advancements in bras that allow every imperfect boob to, at the least, appear perfect!

What was most surprising to me, was how quickly I was able to jump back into normal activities. I was so grateful to have my dad and brother in town. Having all three of us together was grand, but part of me felt like a sheep crying wolf. They had come into town to support me, and I didn't need any supporting, per se. I've always been fiercely independent, to a fault. And I found myself suddenly having the urge to show off my bandages and bruises so I could prove I had surgery. It was strange. I was extremely grateful for the reprieve from incessant cancer talk—most spurred on by me, but still. When the three of us get together we start talking home improvement, recollections about how perfect we were growing up (ha!), and our constant attempt at one-upping our dad's puns, which, for the record, Can't. Be. Done. My dad is the master of punny, my brother and I got nothing on him! Our time together was brief, but for those few days it was nice to feel normal, laugh a lot, and forget that my adventure was just getting started.

Happy Dance!

Thursday, June 29, 2017

Get on your feet and do a mini happy dance with me!

I just received a call from Dr. Hauer, who had some fantastic news to share with me, and you! My lymph node biopsy was clear, NO cancer present! That means the small mass hadn't yet bought its lymph-node-roundtrip-train-ticket to visit other areas of my body! Woo-hoo!

What's else gives me a reason to dance? The margins, the additional tissue Dr. Hauer took surrounding the mass, also came back clean, meaning he evicted the entire no-good, free-loading piece of cancer! Good riddance.

What does this mean? Great question! I'm not out of the woods, *yet*. I know there's still a high probability I'll have radiation and chemo. Phooey.

Let's pause for a moment, shall we? I realize I just told you I'm cancer free. Woo-hoo. So why the need for additional therapies? I'll deal it to you straight. Our current methods of detecting cancer are good, just not great. By the time the mass in my breast was detected, it had most likely been growing for at least one year. I know, right?! Keep in mind this is why mammograms are so important! Also recognize I was getting yearly exams based on my familial history; thank goodness! Here's the thing, cancer starts as a single cell gone rogue. Medicine doesn't yet have anything to detect a cancer cell that small with an exacting level of certainty. So, although the mass was removed from my breast, it's possible a single itty-bitty cancer cell could have jumped ship and tried to find a new home. And that's where radiation and chemo swoop in to take over; they help to ensure the efforts to rid my body of cancer are exhausted, giving me, or anyone, the best chance of staying cancer free for life.

Here's a quick breakdown of radiation versus chemo: Radiation is used for all kinds of procedures. If you've ever had an X-ray of your teeth or a broken bone, you've experienced the wonder of what low doses of those rays can show us. Pretty cool, right?! When applied to cancer, however, they deliver radiation in high doses to kill cells and shrink tumors. Radiation for breast cancer is very localized and targeted. Just like an X-ray only reveals images of a very selective site, radiation only targets the area where the cancer was found. The intent here is to kill any potential cancer cell lingering nearby that wasn't evicted during surgery. Spoiler alert #1: I'll share later in this adventure where I stand on my relationship with radiation.

Chemo, on the other hand, takes a much broader approach to finding and killing rogue cancer cells. Chemo specifically designated for breast cancer can be delivered in several forms but employs a very indiscriminate method of hunting down and killing any fast-growing cells, hence the reason people lose their hair. Spoiler alert #2: my relationship with chemo is forthcoming, stay tuned.

Lastly, I'm still awaiting the results of the genetic testing. Depending upon the insights they return, my doctor may encourage me to undergo additional surgery.

But today . . . we do the HAPPY DANCE!

Get up and move that body, give someone a high five, sing at the top of your lungs to your favorite song, let the sun kiss your face, and be grateful that we're both alive and kickin'.

Until tomorrow, kisses and booty shaking to you!

Penny "Gonna Party Like It's 1999" Casselman

And dance I did! I don't remember what songs played; it didn't matter. All that mattered was that day, in that moment, I was cancer free. I was normal. I was back to my old self as if nothing had happened. The happiness and lightness I felt reminded me how much I had missed dancing. Growing up, I took jazz, tap, and ballet. Not only did I love putting on sparkly outfits and performing but I also loved learning the routines, practicing at home, and being the pupil the teachers would point to for everyone else to mimic.

Sadly, after my mom died, so did my participation in organized dancing. Even though I didn't have classes to attend, I'd still put on my recital leotards until I grew too big to fit in them anymore, and I'd make up my routines in the living room. The most popular artist to dance to—Barry Manilow. Ahh, "Copacabana." In high school, I was captain of the flag team and dance squad—routines galore! Then, years later, in college and through most of my twenties all we did was dance. We danced at fraternity parties—it didn't matter which one either. Had music? Will dance. We danced in our dorm room when we should have been studying. We hitched a ride with a friend lucky enough to have a car, crammed ourselves all in shoulder to shoulder, and in the dead of winter—no coat, mind you—waited outside to get in as snowflakes danced around us. We'd hop back and forth to keep the blood moving, and once inside we danced in dark, loud, hot techno clubs downtown. I went so often that some of the regulars started to refer to me as "backpack girl." I always wore a tiny black backpack to keep my keys, ID, and money in. This gave my arms and hands full reign of the space around me—and I used that space to the max. Every time I danced as a little girl to a college student, I felt empowered, carefree, and fully present in the moment—and that's exactly what I needed the day I received this news.

PART TWO

Prep, Prep, Prep for All To Come

The Carousel of Change

Beginning May 2017, my life began its ride on the carousel of change, after change, after change—*and* it wasn't predicted to slow down or stop. Looking back, giving myself the grace to accept such radical change was one of my biggest obstacles—bigger than my diagnosis. Everything I knew got yanked up, thrown out, turned upside down, questioned, spun around, and reprioritized. *Everything*. Life became different by necessity. I had to find a way to adapt or I'd forever fight change my entire life. I was never a change maker, a go with the flow, or a spur of the moment kinda gal. My calendar was always full and always planned. Although a portion of my adventure would be scheduled—think treatments, tests, and surgeries—what I'd have to navigate was listening to my body and making the necessary adjustments to do what it needed and not just what I wanted to do. Want and need—two very stark things when it comes to questions in the medical realm.

Drum Roll, Please!

Friday, June 30, 2017

This is going to be brief, we'll see, and a fast stream of info.

It's a holiday weekend, and I've got some July 4th'n to do!

Jumping right in.

I met with my surgeon this morning to go over the findings that I shared with you yesterday—woo-hoo! If you didn't do a happy dance then, do one now. As a side note, I wore my strappy gold sparkly pumps to my appointments! Not sure they went with the gown, but I felt pretty fabulous. Also, since one of my new necklaces wasn't going to be in the doctor's way during my post-surgical review, I left that on too. Yay me!

My genetic testing brought with it confirmation of what my gut was telling me: I've got a malfunctioning BRCA2 gene—which brings with it a much higher risk for breast, ovarian, melanoma, and pancreatic cancers compared to that of the average person. You may vaguely recall a mention of BRCA1 in the news—it's the one

Angelina Jolie inherited from her mother—which is nearly the same as my diagnosis. Although both genes have a similar listing of associated cancers, BRCA2 has a more significant risk associated with pancreatic, melanoma—not usually associated with BRCA1—and male breast cancer. Thank goodness I never did like tanning.[1]

Given all this new information—new to me, anyway—and the fact I have already contracted and evicted a cancer mass (thank you very much and good riddance) I have *lots* of new decisions to make and follow-up appointments to schedule. I'm one to move fast, so, for me, the sooner I can line these up and knock 'em down, the better. Also, although I have some time on my side, Dr. Hauer urged me to make decisions and move within three months to stay ahead of any new breast or ovarian cancer that may appear.

Here is my list of follow-up appointments to make in short order!

General oncologist—To discuss radiation and chemo, both of which may be moot if I elect a more invasive option (i.e., surgery).

GYN-oncologist—To discuss, plan, and schedule removal of my ovaries this is a certain plan of action. You see, right now, there are no useful tests to monitor any ovarian cancer activity until it's too late, so the only course of action is removal, and I'm 100 percent ok with that. I have an appointment in three days, Monday, July 3,

---

[1] You can check out the most up-to-date percentages and average risk levels at https://www.cancer.gov/about-cancer/causes-prevention/genetics/brca-fact-sheet as reported by the National Cancer Institute.

to meet and plan with a doctor. Told you I don't waste any time.

Plastic surgeon—To discuss details involved with a bilateral mastectomy and reconstruction. This is a decision I have to weigh in on after I speak with my general oncologist. There are a lot of percentages to weigh and what-ifs to consider along with my overall gut feeling on how to proceed. Don't get me wrong, I'd *love* a *free* boob job (Yes, I said it!), but to be honest, this is a HUGE (no pun intended) surgery that, in itself, comes with risks.

Dermatologist—This is just for a good old "body scan" to help ensure I'm monitoring any abnormalities on my skin, especially since I'm now identified to have a higher risk of melanoma. To be honest, I have so many moles/freckles I routinely schedule yearly body scans with a dermatologist, and I'd like to stay proactive and ahead of anything concerning.

That's it in a nutshell; smaller than a brazil nut, larger than a pistachio, I'm going with a "cashew sized overview." They're my most favorite of the three anyway.

Until next week—lots more updates to come.

Enjoy your holiday weekend.

Penny "Your Human Sparkler" Casselman

Elizabeth, my genetic counselor, confirmed what I had assumed was the case—I had indeed inherited a malfunctioning BRCA2 gene, often referred to as one of the breast cancer genes. I was slightly baffled. Neither my maternal grandmother nor my two maternal aunts had contracted breast cancer, and because of this fact, most doctors had assumed my mom was a mutation case, a one-off in a family. I immediately started to think, "Who did I get this from?" It was a fifty-fifty chance, really. Mom or Dad. I, of course, had my suspicions. Together, Elizabeth and I went through her four pages of prepared genetic handouts detailing all stats associated with my BRCA2 diagnosis. I wasn't prepared to hear about all the other cancers I'm predisposed to. As if battling breast cancer wasn't enough, I'd now have to be forever vigilant for a myriad of other cancers too. With this news, my immediate surgical necessities had doubled. My boobs were obviously not enough to deal with, and now I would have the distinct pleasure of evicting the ovaries too. Are you kidding me? The more, the merrier? I thought to myself, "Can we slow down a bit? I can only deal with one malady at a time, please." Sigh. I took all the information Elizabeth provided in stride. Unlike the breast cancer I was in the process of evicting, there was no evicting a malfunctioning gene—I would have to find a path forward, one of acceptance, vigilance, and grace.

Cry Me a River

Thursday, July 6, 2017

Yep, today I cried a river. Or two. Or three. Sigh.

It's six p.m., and I'm ready to put on jammies and crawl in bed; but first a few quick tasks, then dinner, then maybe some mindless TV so I don't wake up at two a.m. trying to figure out how to get back to sleep.

Today, while sitting in yet another exam room waiting to meet with a doctor to discuss, plan, strategize, and schedule my treatment, the MASSIVE wave of overwhelm hit me hard. Questions like, Am I talking to the doctors in the right order? Am I asking the right questions? Why do I have to quarterback all of this? Why can't this be done already? Why now? Why me?

A roll of the dice, really.

Monday, July 3, I met with the GYN-oncologist, Dr. Resnick, she's very personable and action-oriented, both traits I appreciate. I like her as she seems to have the same laser-focused approach that I do. She'll be the one removing my ovaries; I did get confirmation this will be performed laparoscopically, smile.

You might be wondering why the smile? I mean, it's still surgery, right? Correct. Laparoscopically means they can perform the entire surgery through several very small incisions, think half an inch each, instead of making one large incision approximately six to eight inches long. Some of the benefits include smaller external scars, shorter recovery time, and less pain as you heal. In my book, all three are cause for smiles and celebration.

> Conversely, *mega* sad face that I'll have to immediately deal with menopause; no transition for me. I went cold turkey, no pun intended, when I became a vegetarian, so I guess I can go cold turkey on this too. Not like I have a choice anyway.
>
> Today I met with Dr. Joseph, and I liked her from the get-go. She's professional, seems whip smart, and has a very agreeable bedside manner; all that combined and in my book she's pretty swell! During our visit, Dr. Joseph reached out to my medical oncologist (Dr. Hergenroeder. I'll get to meet him next Thursday.) to discuss some high-level thoughts for the order of the next steps. It appears that right now I'll have chemo first and surgeries late fall.
>
> You keeping up with all these doctors' names and titles? There's a quiz at the end. Just kidding, maybe.
>
> Tomorrow I have a pelvic ultrasound to check in on the health of my ovaries and make sure they haven't welcomed any of their own rogue cells over the years.

Here are some overarching truths I can share right now:

- I will NOT receive radiation. Can I get a woo-hoo?!
- I will receive chemo.
- I will have my ovaries and fallopian tubes removed. For you curious folk, the medical term is salpingectomy-oophorectomy.
- I will have a bilateral mastectomy. Bilateral is the correct medical term. Most laypeople—me included—refer to it as a "double mastectomy" since, to my non-medically geared brain, both boobs are being removed. Learn something new every day, I say!
- I will have breast reconstruction. Notice I didn't say enhancement—there will be nothing to enhance since every part of them is being removed. Yep, all my breast tissue is being scooped out and tossed aside. I'm not looking to go through this chemo and surgery experience again—fingers crossed—so the more they take, the better I feel about being cancer free for the rest of my life.

Truth? I'm exhausted. My eyes are dry and red. And I'm on the verge of being hangry. All of those things combined, and it's good that I have the evening to myself.

Lastly, some random notes:

- I'm happy—yes, happy—to report my cancer is Stage 1.

- My pretty manila folder with all my notes, medical information, and hospital instructions are migrating to a three-ring binder; there are too many papers to keep track of and reference as the process unfolds. This binder is grounding for me as it provides some sense of control—if there is such a thing when evicting cancer.
- My new sparkly necklace has arrived. It's quite spectacular.

As a point of reference, cancer is graded by stages and can range from 0–4; the higher the number the more advanced the cancer is.[2] I was elated to hear mine registered at a 1; it means I've got a much higher chance of living a long, happy, and healthy cancer-free life once all my infusions, surgeries, and therapies are complete. Insert a big sigh of relief.

Office supply stores are one of my favorite places to wander, second only to my love for home improvement warehouses. Who knew I'd get to unleash my organizational prowess during this adventure? At every appointment, I was given a summary of my visit along with upcoming appointments and procedures. In addition, I was also provided a litany of paperwork explaining what I could expect from my treatments and surgeries. When my manila folder failed to expand any further, I knew it was time to bring out the mac-daddy of organization, a big three-ring binder. I found it extremely helpful to separate my boob paperwork from my infusion paperwork from my appointment reminders and visit summaries. I was becoming dizzy sifting through all the sheets of paper trying to find the most recent for the topic in question. I'm a huge fan of the touch-it-once rule for medical paperwork. As

---

[2] Check out https://www.breastcancer.org/symptoms/diagnosis/staging for additional information on the different stages of breast cancer.

soon as I got home and felt well enough to deal with said piece of paper, I'd determine exactly where it needed to go, punch the holes, and put it away. Knowing I still had more than a year of cancer adventures to go, it was this one small piece that helped me worry less, stay sane, and feel in control.

To wrap this up:

> Knowledge is power.
> Ignorance is bliss.
> Yes, to both.
> If I haven't told you yet today, *you are amazing*!

I wouldn't want to be going down this path without you by my side.

> Hugs and kisses.
> Penny "Pensive to a Fault" Casselman

I'm in the Club!

Thursday, July 13, 2017

Check out the sweet swag I got as a welcome gift as I was admitted to the Cancer Care Center Club. Envious much?

- A blue nylon draw-string backpack with which I can carry my binder to and from appointments for reference. I could also stash inside a coloring book, or a sparkly necklace, or a second pair of heels, the sky's the limit!
- A water bottle to remind me to stay hydrated!
- A thermometer so I can monitor my temperature during chemo. In the case of a fever spike (100.4 degrees or higher), I'm instructed to call a doctor immediately or find the nearest ER.

So much info to share. I'll piecemeal it to you over the next few days as a solid sit-down-data-dump requires more attention than I have right now and would, most likely, overwhelm you with too much information to absorb and process.

I remember often feeling helpless when a close friend of mine was going through a health crisis. Unless she or her family explicitly asked me, I just kinda felt at a loss as to what I could do. I don't like asking for help, so I hesitated to put out the request for dinner for the days I have a chemo infusion but thought it would be a way to take some stress off of me (and Joe) and allow others to participate in my adventure! So, I updated my shared calendar and identified dates where you can volunteer for dinner drop off; thank you, in advance, from the bottom of my stomach, I mean heart. As time goes on, I may find I need additional assistance with things, but right now, I'll start with that.

I said it before and I'll say it again: asking for help with dinner on chemo days was the Best. Decision. Ever. For twelve weeks, I was guaranteed to see a friend each week. They felt helpful. I felt grateful. *And* I didn't have to think about what I was going to eat on chemo days and had leftovers to enjoy! The meal drop-offs were a welcomed event I looked forward to. A stark contrast to my feelings in the morning when getting up and going to receive chemo—an event that would have me at the hospital nearly six hours each time. Although the feeling of lethargy greeted me each chemo morning, my mood immediately improved when I crossed the threshold of the Cancer Care Center. Why? Because the staff was kind, caring, sweet, and funny, and they had become my friends. That's my takeaway from this intense time in my adventure—friends make everything better. Their hugs gave me comfort. Their words made me smile. Their thoughts brought me peace. To all of mine—I am forever grateful.

So here we go with the cancer update.

Results of my pelvic ultrasound: all is good under the hood!

They did identify several ovarian cysts; however, they could *clearly* identify them as such without hesitation (i.e., they aren't cancer; woo-hoo!). Therefore, no immediate cause for concern from the GYN side of things.

I also had a meeting with Dr. Hergenroeder today. There were a few special highlights from the visit: I can *finally* pronounce his name with ease! *I didn't cry!* And although I didn't wear my sparkly heels—stupid weather—I did wear my shiny silver Chucks!

I digress.

My appointment went great! I received *lots* of useful info if learning about how long your therapy is going to last and when your hair will fall out is your kind of "good info." Right now for me, that's a resounding yes.

My Taxol (the proper medical name for my chemo) infusions will be administered once a week for twelve weeks starting July 31. This is the therapy that *will* have me losing all my hair. Yep, I'm going to be bald from about August 14 to early December. "Peach fuzz" should start to appear in late December or early January; guess I know what Santa is bringing me for Christmas . . . HAIR! I'm still wrapping my head around this, no pun intended, and I'm not sure how I'm going to address the loss. Stay tuned!

My Herceptin infusions (a monoclonal antibody—there's your word for the day!) will also start on July 31; however, they will only be administered every three weeks. But, here's the kicker, this therapy lasts for an *entire year*! Sigh. Bright side, this therapy does NOT impact my hair growth, so *yay*![3]

Based on the cadence of my infusions (over a year), Taxol's effect of discoloring my veins for a prolonged time if I choose to have it administered in my arm (ick), the number of times I'm going to have to have blood drawn, the numerous surgeries I'm looking at, AND the fact my delicate veins like to conveniently disappear when I get cold, I've opted for a venous port. It will be "installed" on Tuesday, July 25. This port will provide the nurses and doctors easy access to my blood supply and will give me a break from having to get poked and prodded in the arm over and over and over and over and over, you get it, again. Note this will remain UNDER my skin and, other than a bump, won't be visible from the outside.

If you made it this far, you get a *gold star*! Even I'm tired from typing so much. I'll share more personal details with you in the days to come, but these are the BIG overarching medical details, for now.

xoxo

Penny "No Carpal Tunnel, Yet" Casselman

---

[3] Since I'd fumble through the medical description for Taxol and Herceptin, you can find their specifics at Chemocare.com (supported by the Cleveland Clinic). For reference, I had a HER2 positive cancer mass. Only about 20 percent of people with BRCA2 test positive for this—you know I just *had* to be unique.

Happy Boobsday, I Mean Tuesday!

Tuesday, July 18, 2017

Today was my plastic surgeon meet and greet with Dr. Kaufman. A calm and self-assured doc, just what I expected from a plastic surgeon. No white doctor coat here. He wore well-polished loafers, funky socks, Harry Potter-esque trifocals, and a crisp white button-down shirt (sans tie) with two buttons open.

A caveat, I was curious where the term "plastic" surgeon came from, and here's what I found: The word *plastic* in plastic surgery comes from the word *plastikos*, which is Greek for "to mold." And it got this name because plastic surgery involves manipulating and moving tissue around to suit a specific purpose. Insert music and shooting stars, "The more you know."

Our conversation was excellent. I have yet another bundle of paperwork to review, including a ninety-two-page spiral-bound book that addresses numerous questions about reconstructive breast surgery like complications, clinical study results, surgical considerations, follow-up exams, and illustrations of surgical incision points and a breast anatomy overview. Perfect timing as I was just thinking, "What book should I queue up for my next leisurely summer read?"

At this point in my adventure, I'm so numb to people asking me to take off my shirt and don a hospital gown that I'm half tempted to just walk around topless most of the time. I jest, I jest. But maybe I should purchase a few hospital gowns for my personal use and start incorporating them into my daily options of dress.

My breasts had their pictures taken from multiple angles, for posterity sake, which will be used as a guide and reference for Dr. Kaufman when my reconstruction begins, late in 2017. The nurse held a lovely cobalt-blue backdrop while my boobs took center stage for the photo op. I wanted the spring field scene (think school pictures circa 1978), but alas, that option was not available. Ha!

During my visit, I got to hold two different implantable "breasts" in my hand to get a "feel" for them and acquaint myself with the options I have available. Round or molded? Smooth or textured? Big or little? Silicone or saline? To be fair, we also discussed flap procedures—also known as autologous tissue reconstruction (whoa is right!)—which, in essence, uses tissue found elsewhere in your body and relocates it to recreate your boobs.[4] Although it "sounds" like an option to consider, the biggest drawback is a potential

---

[4] You can visit https://www.cancer.org/cancer/breast-cancer/reconstructionsurgery/breast-reconstruction-options/breast-reconstruction-using-yourown-tissues-flap-procedures.html to learn about the different types of flap procedures available.

loss of muscle range in the affected removal area and a scar at every harvest location. *No thanks!* One decision made thank you very much.

To my dad, brother, cousins, and guy friends, thanks for managing through all this boob talk! Didn't mean to prompt images of your daughter, sister, cousin, friend that you now can't wipe from your memory or undo, but I know you all knew I was a woman and had these as part of my composition anyway.

Tomorrow is my breast MRI; yeesh, these girls have more photo ops than I do!

Still doesn't feel real as nearly everything lately has been *talking* about what's *going* to happen, not *doing* anything about moving the process along. I realize that's all about to change, starting next week, and get REAL.

That's all for now—happy boobsday, I mean Tuesday.

xo

Penny "So Many Options, So Little Time" Casselman

It did feel surreal. Doctor appointments after doctor appointments, yet nothing was happening. I had my initial surgery, and the cancer mass was gone. I felt fine. I looked good. Just busy with appointments. I suppose that made things easier—I was going through the motions like a good soldier. Stay focused; do what they say. I'd already navigated grad school for three straight years while holding down a full-time job, so this seemed a little too easy. But what lie ahead for me was far more intense than any final exam or group presentation I had ever faced. But like all other obstacles I'd encountered before, I'd face it head-on and figure out all the details along the way.

Where Does the Time Go?

Friday, July 21, 2017

If you're on Facebook or Pinterest, I know you've had a similar feeling. You hop on "for just a minute" and ninety minutes later, you look around asking yourself, "What just happened?!" Yeah, I just did that. I sat down over an hour ago to write an update, and then I started looking online at "cancer head coverings." *Ugh*. Then I discovered I was hungry and had to grab food; I'm notorious for losing track of time and dismissing any hunger pangs until, yep, I get *hangry*.

A swift update today.

My breast MRI on Wednesday went fine. I've had an MRI before and was prepared for the noise. However, I didn't fully understand how it was all going to play out, seeing as how I had to lay face down on the MRI table, motionless, for an hour, *with* my breasts going commando and hanging freely down. My face down pose could be best described as Superman flying drunk. My arms were stretched out in front of me, boobs hung on either side of a partition, and my knees slightly bent to relieve any stress on my back; my feet dangled down off the end of the table. I nearly fell asleep but forced myself to open my eyes so I wouldn't make the "jerky sleep move" I sometimes do right before I fall asleep. Any movement meant I'd have to be repositioned and start all over—yikes. I'm happy to report that I did *great*!

Right before I was taken back for my procedure, I received a call from an oncology nurse letting me know I'd need to find a lab for some pre-port blood work. I figured I was already out and about, had the time to spare, and was still in possession of a good arm/vein to poke, so off I went to another facility to donate. I wish I were double fisting a craft cocktail rather than double cotton pads in the crook of my elbow on that Wednesday afternoon. Another time!

I received my results back yesterday, and everything looked normal (i.e., they didn't see any tiny cancer masses they might have missed in the right breast, where the surgery took place, or in the left breast and left lymph nodes). *Yay!*

Have a stellar weekend.
Peace and love!
Penny "Super Woman" Casselman

Echo, Drain, and Port

Tuesday, July 25, 2017

ECHO. My echocardiogram went fine. No news yet as to results, but I'm always of the opinion that no news is good news. Thankfully, no needles for this procedure, and I got to keep my pants and shoes on!

DRAIN. I had a pleasant discussion with Dr. Joseph's APRN-CNP[5], Anna, about upcoming appointments and asked her about lymphedema and the need to avoid my right arm, now and forever. Anna confirmed that I should, going forward, avoid any activity in my right arm. Activity in this sense relates to blood draws, IVs, blood pressure cuffs, and such as my lack of a full assortment of lymph nodes on the right side has the potential to cause lymphedema, which is an awful condition that, although not permanent, is disfiguring and I'd like to avoid. Anna did say they are far more strict with people who have had

---

[5] APRN-CNP stands for advanced practice registered nurse, certified nurse practitioner. Visit https://www.ncsbn.org/aprn.htm for additional details.

all lymph nodes removed and that, since I still have some on that side, I could, if needed, have activity in the arm if there was no other option available.

Today, I worry more about lymphedema than I do about a recurrence of cancer. Crazy, right? What is it? Your lymphatic system is part of your body's immune system and those of us navigating cancer can experience damage to the lymphatic highway when lymph nodes are removed; recall I had five taken out in my first surgery. In a nutshell, it's a build-up of lymphatic fluid under your skin when the fluid is blocked from circulating properly. You can find a lot more details on the Google machine, so I won't bore you here.[6] But lymphedema is something I think about every time I get a twinge near my right armpit. Given my active status and my caution when vitals are taken or blood drawn, I believe I'm in a very low risk category for occurrence. Whew.

PORT. Yep, today was "installation" day. I was awake but opted to accept half a Xanax dose to ease any anxiety during the procedure. It went fine. A little disconcerting at times—I won't go into details as I know some of you might pass out or have to sit down—but I now have two stitched up incision points, two more badges of warrior honor, I suppose. Although most people have a port installed on their right side, under the collar bone, mine was installed on the left since my right side is still recovering from my lumpectomy and sentinel lymph node removal. You know me, though, always got to be special.

---

[6] To learn more about lymphedema, this website https://www.cancer.org/treatment/treatments-and-sideeffects/physical-side-effects/lymphedema/what-is-lymphedema.html provides a comprehensive overview.

I came home and took a three-hour nap. I'm still a little sore and tight in the area, but I know my discomfort will pass and can be managed with Tylenol. I'm a bit apprehensive about sleeping tonight, as I'm a stomach sleeper and I *know* that won't be happening. Baby steps back to normal.

That's all for now.

More in the days to come.

Hugs, kisses, and love to you.

Penny "the *Former* Human Pincushion" Casselman

I didn't fully grasp how visible this little port was going to be. I even received the low profile one and can't fathom what the regular profile one must look like. Since my port was installed on the left side of my chest, for the entire summer of 2017, I was reminded of what I was going through every single time I got in the car to drive and put on my seatbelt. And again when I slung my crossbody handbag over my left shoulder. To ease the discomfort of the seatbelt, I purchased a fuzzy black seat belt wrap so the seatbelt and port could be friends and play nice together while I drove. I also trained myself to swing my bag across my right shoulder, something I still do today. Two years later, in 2019, my port was still hanging around.

Got My Wig(s) ON!

Saturday, July 29, 2017

Today was my appointment in the wig salon, 10:00 a.m. sharp!

I had fun because, right now, I knew I could still go back to my hair when I was done "playing" with the wigs, but not for long.

In the past, any wigs I owned were always a prop for my Halloween costume. Alas, today's selections would need to reflect the real me, on the daily, not some pretend character I was morphing into for the evening. I didn't want any of the wigs, but I was going through the motions. I had to remind myself that this (impending hair loss) was happening, and with that, I let Sandra, the manager of the salon, impart her wisdom of wigs to me.

I must have tried on twenty of them in various shades of red, blonde, strawberry blonde, and brunette. Why not have some fun with this, right? Within those color pallets, I tried styles of long, short, straight, and curly. I whittled my selection down to three, and then to the final two. Sandra liked my sass and thought I looked so good in the final two options that she sent me home with both! I'm thinking the silvery-white, poker-straight bobbed wig with blunt bangs will be for wild nights out on the town or holidays like Thanksgiving, Christmas, and New Year. Think of how good a sparkling barrette would look among the locks?! I know, right?! And my short brunette pixie cut will be for everyday errands like grocery shopping and pumping gas.

Each wig has a perch in my bedroom atop a carefully crafted stand. Long gone are the days of storing wigs on white Styrofoam heads like my mom used. I've got a modern silver stand and my porcelain red gloss bust of Buddha! I'm still not sure if Buddha looks better in the brunette pixie cut or the sassy silver number; the jury is still out.

I went to brunch immediately after the appointment and wore the pixie cut wig! I figured now is as good a time as any to test the waters and see how it felt on me, and me in it. Sitting at the MOST prominent table at First Watch—seriously, it was the only table open and could have seated six—I pulled out my chair and plopped down. No one even batted an eyelash; trust me, I was scanning the entire restaurant. "Ok," I said to myself, "I can do this." Honestly, the whole time I sat there, I felt like I was wearing a baseball cap. Despite my unfortunate genetic makeup, I do have several things going for me headed (no pun intended . . . well, maybe) into this hair loss adventure: First, I've always looked good in hats, but I recognize not everyone feels as lucky. Although to be fair, I believe everyone can look good in a hat if you try on enough of them, I digress. Second, I routinely wear baseball hats, especially on the weekend, so my feeling of wearing a "hat" didn't faze me.

It was, however, *itchy*! Even donning my best Halloween wig, I can usually only get through about four hours of wearing it. It *may* be less itchy when all my hair falls out, since today I had my real hair slicked back, tied in a ponytail, tucked under a nylon hair cap, and my wig on top of all of that. One thing is for sure, wearing a wig *is* like wearing a hat, I think I'll be quite toasty this winter.

Having talked about wigs this entire post, I'm not sure I'll wear one that often. I know it's not my hair, and so does everyone else who knows me, so why fake it? Maybe I'll really like being bald or having a shaved head? I do plan on getting scarves and head wraps, so perhaps I'll prefer more of that type of cue ball cover? Time will tell, and it'll be here sooner than I want.

All in all, it was a good day, and that's all I can ask for!

Peace, love, and long luscious locks to you!

xo

Penny "To Hat, or Not to Hat" Casselman

Oh YES. I. DID.

Sunday, Jul 30, 2017

I did it. Why wait, ya' know?!

Originally on my calendar for Thursday, August 10, it happened at nine p.m. on Sunday, July 30. What's eleven more days in the grand scheme of things?

Honestly, I was tired of thinking about it. I was tired of wondering when all my hair was going to fall out. Wondering if I should cut it on the 10th or do it on the 9th or maybe the 11th. Or should I push the boundaries and wait until the 12th? Rebel!

NOPE.

I figured doing it now would be the first step for me transitioning to being utterly hair free, seeing as I still have hair all over my head, albeit very, very, very short.

I wasn't born with a thick head of hair. It's the only baby feature I never outgrew. My mom had the same hair texture. I pondered the decision to cut my hair for days, it consumed my every waking moment. Each time I looked in the mirror I'd imagine what I'd look like bald. Not only was I convinced my skull was lumpy and uneven, something I wasn't ready to show the world, I also didn't want everyone I encountered to treat me like I was a cancer patient. Even though I was, it wasn't their right to assume anything. Turns out my skull isn't lumpy after all, just feels that way to me, I digress.

For the guys out there, I went with a #2. I did most of the cutting myself as I wanted to be in control of the loss, but Joe did have to step in to ensure I didn't miss any of the hairs on the very back of my head.

I also freed up some space on my counter as every single styling product—six unique bottles, if you must know—and hair accessory was tucked neatly away; I clearly won't need any of them again until sometime in 2018.

I've had the clippers for quite a while since I routinely shaved the back of my hair myself—I like a tight undercut. Yes, I'm quite talented. So my decision to cut all my hair off didn't require me to leave the house, make an appointment, or purchase any new equipment.

Did I cry? Yes, but *way less* than I was expecting, maybe because I didn't realize how cute I'd be without hair. Ha! Figured I'd reserve the crying for tomorrow when it *really gets real*, and I have to sit at the main hospital campus while chemo drips slowly through my veins for hours, sigh.

Make no mistake, I'm still going to lose every single little strand of baby-fine hair remaining on my head and will be left with a shiny, uber-smooth noggin' for many, many months. This is just a stepping-stone for me to acclimate to my new reality.

With a buzz buzz here, and a buzz buzz there.
xo
Penny "A Barber I Am Not" Casselman

If someone had asked me in April of 2017 to shave my head for a million dollars, I'm quite confident I would have turned them down. Thinking back, that sure does put a lot of things in perspective, no? Hair? I'd say today with reckless abandon, "It grows back, who cares?! Now give me that million dollars." I do enjoy having hair to style again. I've kept it short which makes my life so much easier than my previous blonde streaked, undercut, asymmetrical style that I used to wear pulled up a majority of the time anyway—but not before I put styling cream on it and blow-dried it. I snicker at all the fuss I used to make over my hair. Looking back at the pictures when I thought my hair was pulled back, tight, and looking good, I looked bald anyway. HA!

Image provided courtesy of Tom J. Noe Photography

PART THREE
Chemo

A Solid Routine

I've never experienced a broken bone. Quick, knock on a piece of wood! I know people who've had broken bones. I've seen casts on arms, legs, and feet. I've heard stories of how annoying a cast is. Although I can empathize with someone going through the bone healing process, I just don't know what I don't know; same went for chemo. I was given all kinds of materials to review, preparing me for what I may experience, but until I climbed in the seat and the first drip started, I had no idea how I, or my body, would react. Twenty-twenty hindsight what it is, they were pretty spot on with several warnings, though there were other potential hazards I escaped. In chemo, as in life, every person is unique.

I found a solid routine over the course of twelve weeks, and referring to them as groundhog weeks is fitting. Since Mondays were my assigned chemo days, I'd look forward to events later in the week and through the weekend—things like friends visiting and running mundane errands—as each gave me a sense of normalcy. When friends visited, the topic of cancer was always being discussed, and I was happy to participate. It gave me comfort in two ways: First, it meant the person I was talking to had a genuine interest in what I was going through, and second, it allowed me to showcase my cancer expertise. Although, cancer is one expertise I'd be happy to forfeit.

Snow White, Sleepy

Monday, July 31, 2017

    I am so tired! Holy cow! The dose of Benadryl they started me with, and will continue to administer before each subsequent chemo infusion, was a doozy! There is no way I could drive home after this, as I'd fall asleep at the wheel. Thank goodness Chauffeur Joe is at my disposal today.

    The Benadryl did a few things:

1. Helped my body not to reject the Taxol. Yay, it worked!
2. It made me super-duper sleepy!
3. My dose was so high that the arch of my foot, soles of my feet, and lower calf were quite spazzy. Not in a pins-and-needles kinda way or a painful way. I can describe as that feeling you get right before you sneeze but never sneeze! Thank goodness that halfway through my Taxol therapy, about thirty-five minutes, it did subside. Whew!!

I'm writing this still hooked up to my IV and I'm nearly finished with this first round! I wanted to drop you a quick note since I'll probably fall asleep on the ride home and then hop in bed for some quality nappy-nap time.

I did great today if I do say so myself!

I did not cry (not that there's anything wrong if I had).

I rocked my new haircut, without hesitation. No wig today!

My port was *fantastic*, and it only took the nurse one attempt to access it, yay!

Thank you for all your warm wishes, support, and wildly positive vibes; they certainly worked.

Who knows what tomorrow holds, how I'll feel in a day or so, or how the next infusion will affect me. Just one day at a time.

Stay tuned for more updates as the days progress.

Drip, drip, *beep!*

xo

Penny "I'm Ready for Nap Time" Casselman

Drip, drip, BEEP indeed! These new and annoying sounds echoed up and down the chemo halls All. Day. Long. A soft rhythmic clicking and ticking emanated from the machines that monitored the chemo infusion. At the start of each session, the assigned nurse programmed them to administer my dose over a precise amount of time. Too fast, and I risk feeling sick. Too slow, and my patience begins to vanish as I realize the amount of time I've lost by sitting in a moss-green pleather chair that would only maintain its recline position if you weighed over three hundred pounds. I never did experience a sustained recline during any of my infusions, but my arms and core certainly got a workout at the start of every session. I was sure that one day I would be assigned the single chair that would actually relent to my efforts and provide me with a first-class recline I was so hopeful of enjoying. Eternal hope springs forth, but it never happened.

The beeping was the piercing sound which signaled one of two things, the timer had caused the drip to stop or the fluid drip had reached its conclusion. More often than not, it was the timer that had concluded, and usually, there were still a few micro-ounces of chemo remaining in the bag. The nurses would scurry over to silence the incessant beeping. I have to believe that beeping was as shrill and ear-piercing to them as it was for those of us sitting immediately beside the machine. More likely, it was nothing more than the nurses' "child" in the cancer wing—as if yelling, "Mom, Mom, Mom!" ad nauseam. Luckily, any nurse could come to my rescue, not just Chris—my assigned nurse—thank goodness. More often than not, the nurse would have to throw on a few more minutes to ensure I'd receive every last drop of my precious poison. My bag was flat as a pancake and bone dry at the end of every appointment—I appreciated the thoroughness of the nurses. At times there would be three or four machines all beeping at the same time—of course, it always seemed to happen when I was fast asleep dreaming of lipstick and high heels.

It helped to have a morning checklist to reference each chemo day—especially since I knew I'd be at the hospital for a minimum of six hours. Included in my list were the following items, listed here in order of importance:

1. Blanket
2. Neck pillow
3. iPad
4. Juice
5. Snacks
6. Lunch

7. Water bottle
8. iPhone

Although the chair recline was just as elusive as an uninterrupted and deep sleep, I was able to cobble together a little routine for the day which helped me feel as if I was in control of what was happening.

One Down, Eleven to Go

Wednesday, August 2, 2017

Of chemo infusions, that is.

Monday night was AWFUL; if I got four hours of sleep, it was a miracle, and those hours were not consecutive. Duty called, however, and I was back at the hospital at eight a.m. Tuesday morning for my seven-day post-port-placement follow-up. All is good. My incision is looking great, there's no sign of infection, the stitches successfully dissolved, and despite some bruising, no more attention is needed port-wise.

I took a nap on Tuesday and went to bed early. Although I still have bouts of tiredness during the day, I felt pretty normal. *Yay!* My appetite is good, and I haven't noticed any other chemo-induced changes thus far. Potential differences that may begin to appear include sensitivity to smells, dry skin, changes in my taste profile, and lots more hair loss, *of course*!

I also have to be extremely careful in the sun—as if being fair wasn't cause enough—since chemo can make a girl like me crisp up pretty quickly. Luckily, I wear a daily sunscreen anyway but will be stepping up my game with higher SPF if I go out. Hats and long sleeve shirts will also aid in shielding from the solar rays.

It's hard for me to fathom the decimation that is running rampant in my system right now. I still have hair, lashes, and brows. I'm eating fine. My skin is ok. I look and feel normal other than my slight fatigue. What I keep envisioning is the ad for Lamisil; you know, the one featuring those little diggers? I envision I have my own contingent of little diggers going after my hair follicles and every other quick dividing cell; yes, you can hate me now for putting that image in your head! I know it's necessary and that, in due time, chemo—and all its decimation—will cease. It's strange to think everything I'm going through is voluntary. *I know right?!* Yes, yes, yes, I'm *happily* going through this so that I'm on the other side living a long, happy, and healthy life!

This week I received my shipment of three head coverings, and I love them all! Although I'm happy to tool around town in my new buzzed look, I realize that I *will* need head coverings as the months pass. They won't be worn because I'm embarrassed by my naked head or my lack of hair, but more for warmth and an additional pinch of flair.

Yesterday, I went to Starbucks and ran into one of my favorite baristas, Robert, who looked at me and just smiled and chatted as usual. Robert shaves his head and I joked I wanted to be as cool as him! It made me feel good that life is still plugging away as usual—long hair, short hair, or no hair.

It's one day at a time, and, so far, they've been good days.

Thank you for the continued good vibes, well wishes, encouraging words, prayers, and healing thoughts; I feel them all and accept them without hesitation!

Much love to you
Penny "Sinead" O'Casselman

3/16" is SHORT

Sunday, August 13, 2017

    I knew when I buzzed my hair down to a #2, back on July 30, this day would come. That before my hair would give up its good fight to hold on, I'd need a haircut! I kid you not. My hairs were starting to drive me batty so today I grabbed the clippers once more and took the noggin sprouts down to 3/16", holy cow is that short! You see, I want as little hair as possible letting go and making a mess in my bed, in the shower, or in the hallway. Who knows where or how my hair will fall out, but I do know the timing. The first question I asked Dr. Hergenroeder when we met was, "When is my hair falling out?" He calmly and succinctly returned the response, "Week three." My friends, this is my week three.

    I envision the commentary on my hair loss to go something like this: Today, the eastern part of the US, Greenland, and the southern tip of Africa exited the "Casselman Sphere"; rumblings are starting that Antarctica, Great Britain, Mexico, and Canada may soon follow suit. All I know—I don't want to clean up hairs for days on end, so I'm hopeful the falling-out process is fast and efficient.

To ensure I'm prepared should the loss occur while I'm out and about, I now carry one of my hats at all times in my handbag along with a few tabs of my anti-nausea medication. I haven't been nauseous at all yet; however, I'm told that week three, in addition to being the week I'll lose my hair, may also be the week that other symptoms may start to arise, like changes in smell and taste.

Just like a dandelion releasing its seeds, so to goes your hair. Think of it this way, to release its seeds, a dandelion requires a nudge from some external force—the wind, the vibration of a stem being picked, or a squirrel running by in a flurry. Yes, most people report losing their hair in the shower or in bed; both are places where your head is moving around causing your hair to experience tugging and highly active movement. I knew there was always the possibility of my hair departing if I scratched my head, tried on a shirt at the store and pulled it over my head, or simply rested my head on the headrest in the car. I like to be prepared, and so I was.

I'm trying not to think too far ahead, as I'm still so early in my adventure, but what I'm going through now is easy street compared to the surgeries I have on the horizon. Honestly, the past two weeks, other than the annoyance of spending no less than half a day at the hospital, have been quite uneventful. No nausea, no mouth sores, no intestinal distress, no changes in taste or smell, no hair loss (other than what I've intentionally brought about), and sleep has been, for the most part, restful enough. I keep waiting for the other shoe to drop but sending every positive vibe out to the universe that all faculties keep their status quo.

Changing gears. Here are a few things I've learned/discovered thus far in my adventure:

1. I'm a better writer than I have ever given myself credit for.
2. Fuzzy lamb-wool seat belt shoulder covers are cozy, comfy, and make me happy.
3. *No one* cares about my hair or lack thereof. NOBODY. *Not. One. Person.* How liberating!
4. I thoroughly enjoy juicing.
5. I *love* my sparkly necklaces!

Here are a few new things I have to look forward to in my adventure:

1. I'm going to become a *master* at two new cosmetic applications: (a) drawing on my eyebrows and (b) applying faux eyelashes.
2. I'll be exploring ways of satisfying my sweet tooth without the addition of processed/refined sugar.
3. I'll discover more activities to support self-care.
4. *More* sparkly necklaces *and* earrings will enter my life!

Tomorrow is round three of twelve as my chemo countdown continues. I do hope this finds you happy, healthy, and enjoying the summer! Cheers to you, my most loyal reader!

xoxo

Penny "Khaleesi" Casselman, First of Her Name, Mother of Sparkle, Liberator of Follicles, and Queen of Juicing

I'm a planner, as you well know by now. And before my adventure went into full-swing, I made some decisions about my health. I was not going to imbibe any alcohol for the twelve weeks of chemo. I figured I was going to be doing enough destruction inside my body and didn't need to tax it any more than was already happening. Following that same train of thought, I would avoid processed sugar when possible.

I also decided that I would embrace the world of juicing. Around 2010 I decided to become vegetarian thanks to the documentary *Forks over Knives* that explored the impact of animal protein on our body chemistry and the potential links to cancer (psst, I'm a science nerd at heart).[7] Attempting to avoid the same fate as my mom and not knowing at the time I was predisposed to cancer given my malfunctioning BRCA2 gene, I didn't think twice about making the leap to a predominately plant based diet. I'd still make the same decision today, regardless. Jump forward about three years and I was introduced to Kris Carr, a wellness activist and cancer thriver. Mind you, I've not personally met her, maybe one day. But I have huge respect for her. It was from the additional insights I gleaned from Kris that I became more focused on improving my health through the food choices I was making. I loved getting fresh juice blends when I was out for brunch or grabbing an afternoon pick-me-up, and I felt cancer had finally given me a permission slip to get a masticating juicer and give it a go for myself. Kris's recipe book[8] was my juicing bible during those twelve weeks. And the juicing experience

---

[7] Check out https://www.forksoverknives.com/ for additional insights and resources related to their plant-based nutritional lifestyle.

[8] Visit https://kriscarr.com to learn more about Kris Carr and her juice recipe book, *Crazy Sexy Juice*. I highly recommend it!

didn't disappoint. I never thought I would enjoy green juice—but man-oh-man is a glass fresh off the press heavenly! Quick note, I'm no saint when it comes to ultra-healthy eating, but I do what I can when it aligns with my beliefs.

Three Minute Miracle

Sunday, August 20, 2017

Tomorrow is the start of chemo week four, and I enter it with, drumroll please, a *full head of hair and eyebrows and eyelashes*! Say what?! It's true!

I'm not sure how I've maintained my luscious locks and peripheral hair, but no need to forcefully question; I don't want to tempt Murphy's Law, ya' know?!

Tomorrow will be a long day at the hospital as both chemo and Herceptin infusions will be administered.

This update is short and sweet, just like my hair.

xo

Penny "Outlier" Casselman

PS, The book of a similar name (*Outliers*) is quite fantastic! I'm a fan of any book by Malcolm Gladwell.

PS-2, No money was exchanged for the Pantene feature.

PS-3, "Don't hate me because I'm beautiful."

PS-4, I crack myself up.

Groundhog Day

Monday, August 28, 2017

Just like that, it's Monday again. My life is now defined by Mondays. I'm sure you often feel the same way, Monday *again*?!

Sunday is my prep day. Travel pillow: check. Blanket: check. iPad: check. Lunch, snack, and juice: check.

This will be my fifth in a series of twelve; seven more chemos to go.

Yesterday, in addition to being prep day, was another haircut! Took it down to a tight #1 this time. You see, on Thursday my hair started to fall out in droves. It was a sad day, and although I knew the day would come, it's an entirely other experience holding the losses in the palm of your hand. Surprisingly, I still have lots of sprouts remaining! They've gone from a fuzzy-wuzzy teddy bear feel to a baby porcupine coat. My hair loss going forward, I'm guessing, will be far less noticeable as the departing length might look more like dust than hair.

This round of hair loss gave me a reason to pull out all my head gear and try them on again—scarves, hats, and even the wigs. They're all much cuter than I remember, yay and fun!

That's all for now. Gotta get in gear to make my appointment this morning.

Cheers to yet another day in the cycle.

Your little groundhog,

Penny "Punxsutawney" Casselman

Flattery Will Get You Far!

Monday, September 4, 2017

I had no idea hospitals closed, ever. This girl, however, caught a break today as the Cancer Care Center was closed in observance of Labor Day! It was nice to have a break in my new routine, and it provided me with a sense of normalcy, albeit brief. Tomorrow, I'm back at it again.

But guess what?! I'll be *halfway through* my chemo infusions! Yay, kinda'. If I'm honest, and really what else is there, it still feels like a lifetime away from me completing this adventure. Yes, chemo is only a twelve-week blip, but I still have Herceptin through July 2018 and my final reconstructive surgery will occur sometime in the fall of 2018 (I'm guessing, nothing is confirmed yet). People, it's only September 2017! There's still plenty of road to trod, paths to follow, detours to experience, and lessons to learn, I'm sure. I try not to think too far ahead as I can only live one day at a time anyway, and I'm trying to avoid heading down a dark rabbit hole of thoughts that, if I'm not careful, can become overwhelming.

Speaking of surgery, last week, I touched base with my oncologist; if you're keeping track, that would be Dr. Hergenroeder. He was impressed that I still have noggin sprouts, stating that it's standard for most people to go entirely bald in week three. There's nothing standard about this gal, but you knew that already. Although I do have hairs left, they are thinning with each passing week, and I fully anticipate that before I hit infusion twelve, I will be a shiny cue ball.

My most pressing question for Dr. Hergenroeder was this, "What's the timing for my surgery?" To my shock, he said, "Whenever you want." Say *what*? You heard it right—whenever I want. I was glad to hear it didn't have to be immediately after I stopped chemo, as I was very hopeful to enjoy the holidays (Thanksgiving, Christmas, and New Year's) without also dealing with recovering from major surgery. So, yay! Having said that, *why* would I want to prolong this adventure? Why would *anyone* want to extend this process? I don't understand, and I digress.

The reason there is no "timeline" is that my surgeries are, in essence, optional. Have no fear; I consider them mandatory because I've looked at the percentages Elizabeth provided that compare my chances of contracting other forms of cancer in contrast to the general population. I have no desire to go through another adventure. Yes, I want to be the healthy old lady in the nursing home with the best boobs! I have no desire to drag this entire process out into 2019, as I'm not sure my cheery disposition could hold out for that long. As of today, my planned course of action is to pursue scheduling my surgeries for January 2018, stay tuned.

Something interesting happened to me Sunday while dining out at Corky & Lenny's—a local deli. As I was waiting at the table for additional guests to arrive, a woman seated at a booth diagonal from me stood up to make her way to the restroom, I assumed. As she was passing the table, she stopped, looked at me, and said, "I hope you don't think this rude, but I noticed . . . that . . . are you?" She looked at me with one of those do-you-know-what-I'm-thinking looks.

I piped up and responded, "Yes, I'm dealing with breast cancer and am currently undergoing chemo."

She then launched into her personal story of breast cancer and on more than one occasion needed to point out, while poking herself in her right breast, that "This one is fake, it's just a gel-filled insert for my bra," and that "When my doctors asked me if I was interested in reconstruction, I looked at them and said, 'I'm seventy-five years old. I don't need that one anymore so just take it off.'"

I responded with, "Well, you look symmetrical." She continued to offer words of encouragement, asked for my name (which I kindly gave her), and she said she'd pray for me every day. I thanked her. Honestly, I thought it was cute—a little weird in the middle of a busy Corky & Lenny's, but sweet—that she felt I looked friendly enough to approach.

On her way out of the restaurant, she stopped again to offer additional words of encouragement and said, "God will take you when he's ready and not before!"

To which her companion piped up and said, "She's just afraid God's going to give her a dust cloth rather than take her." Note: I have no idea what that means.

She also said, "You have a well-shaped head, it suits you, you look good." And off they went. Yes, flattery will get you far!

Until my next update, kisses to you!

Penny "Don't You Look Mah-ve-lous" Casselman

After chemo concluded and my body started to recover from its devastation, I was very cautious with the words I used around other women with super tight haircuts in the Cancer Care Center. I could tell that not every woman going through chemo and experiencing similar hair loss was as embracing of the process as I was. It's odd the line you walk when talking about cancer with other patients. My gauge was always a smile. If I smiled at someone and they smiled back, it was a signal that yes, they were happy to chat. And I usually did. Other times I'd smile, and instead of seeing it reflected back, their eyes would look away or their chin would drop, and I knew they were dealing with their own thoughts and preferred to be quiet—I understood and respected. Somehow, I think they knew my smile was a hug, a way of saying—without words—that you will get through today, it's all we can do.

Out in the "real-world"—yeesh—that's a whole other encounter. I try never to ask the cancer question to someone. My approach is akin to the pregnancy rule. You never ever dare ask, "When are you due?" unless they have revealed their condition to you. I did that once—and only once—to learn that lesson. I'm not about to repeat that with any cancer assumption.

Lately I've noticed a shift in tone toward women with short or buzzed hair. Makeup ads, some fashion spreads, and even Hollywood A-listers are showing off their short locks from a place of beauty, strength, and feminism. Although, it still feels like an exception. Bravo ladies around the world—I support and join you in the short hair revolution!

Growing up, I was conditioned to believe you were one of two things if you had extremely short hair: either a cancer patient or gay. I hate that I said that, gay. Ugh. I have many paradigm shifts to make. Just know I'm a work in progress, on so many levels, and I'm encouraged to see that numerous brands, high-profile individuals, and the general public at large are starting to make those shifts with me.

Twelve Hours

Thursday, September 7, 2017
You're probably thinking one of the following:

1. To what do I owe this pleasure of an update from Penny midweek?
2. Is everything ok? Penny usually only writes a weekly update.
3. What's going to happen in twelve hours?

Fret not, my friend, all is ok.

Twelve hours simply refers to the number of hours I slept last night. *Holy cow* is right and is an appropriate response. Yeesh. I could hardly believe it myself. I guess that's what happens when you sleep five hours Tuesday night and can only manage a one-hour nap Wednesday, your body cries "uncle" and forces you to take a time out.

What a wacky day today. Waking up at eleven a.m. completely throws off timing for the rest of your day!

I showered at five p.m. and was ready to be "productive" at six. Thank goodness the grocery store is open until eight thirty and Target until eleven p.m.! I just couldn't look at the four walls of my house anymore, so off I went to make headway on some errands I thought would have already been accomplished by this time today.

Of course, I now find myself quite alert and not ready for bed, hence my update to you.

As per usual, fall seems to have arrived in Cleveland as fast as flipping a light switch. I'm wearing some form of head covering almost daily because my dainty scalp is chilly! I've also realized I need more options for the noggin and so another order for head coverings will be made in short order. I can't walk around not sporting a coordinated outfit.

Is it weird I don't like pictures of me with hair anymore? Ok, there are a few good pictures of me with hair, but when I look at most of them, I think, "What were you thinking?! You spent how long blow-drying, adding product, bleaching every four weeks, brushing, twirling, adding more product, pulling it back only to wear it down, then clip it back again, finally adding hairspray, and having the wind blow it around again?" Just reading all that and I'm exhausted! The time I would have saved! Having said this, however, I do find I spend more time on my makeup since I don't have any hair to detract from the features that are now front and center, literally! All in all, I'm guessing I spend the same amount of time getting ready now as I did pre-cancer.

I maintain hairs all over my head; however, their numbers continue to dwindle with each passing week. I still have eyelashes and eyebrows, but they might be thinning too. I'm having a harder time discerning precisely what state of affair they're in since the contrast against my hairline is still quite dramatic. Now when I get ready for bed and look at myself in the mirror, I look like an extra from a post-apocalyptic sci-fi movie. Though, that is one of my favorite entertainment genres! Perhaps I've stumbled upon my new profession when this adventure is over? Watch out, Hollywood!

I remind myself every day to stay positive. Yesterday is gone and tomorrow isn't here, so relax. I can only appreciate, enjoy, cherish, and be grateful for the minute I have right now.

Be kind to yourself.

Enjoy the remainder of your week.

Stay tuned for more "deep thoughts" from yours truly.

xoxo

Penny "Jack Handey" Casselman

Pensive

Friday, September 22, 2017

Has it really been two weeks since my last update? Yeesh. My apologies. Does it count that I've thought about providing an update on many occasions?

First off, eight appointments down; that's two-thirds of the way done if you like math. Just four more chemo infusions to go. I'm hanging in there and, if you might have guessed, ready for this part of the adventure to be over.

The cumulative effect of chemo is taking its toll—*dang it*! I was hoping to have escaped neuropathy; however, last week I started to notice it creeping up. Just like everything associated with cancer, the impact varies from patient to patient. For me, it's presenting on my right side and is most pronounced in my right hand. My neuropathy is a very warm tingling sensation and less of a pins and needles type of thing. In case you were wondering, my hand will often feel like when you go outside in the winter without gloves, stay there for a few minutes, find your way back inside, and then immediately decide to wash your hands in warm water. *Wowza!* I'm grateful that it's not pins and needles; however, the warmer the object I touch, the more numb and tingling my hand becomes. Therefore, my showers are less steamy these days, I don't pick up anything hot, and I always wear my Mr. Clean non-latex gloves while doing dishes.[9]

Additionally, I'm finding I have less energy on any given day. I'm bummed. I just want to be spunky-monkey, sparkler, social butterfly, shiny Penny again. I'm kinda feeling lost. I know I'll be back, since you can't keep a good woman down! *But*—four more weeks just seems like a lifetime at this point.

I'm still staying active despite any lull in energy I experience. I go to yoga every Saturday morning at the Gathering Place. And today, after more than ten years of living in Shaker Heights, I *finally* went to the Nature Center at Shaker Lakes and took a nice long walk on one of their many paths. It was quite lovely and indeed an activity I'll be partaking in more often.

I'm also doing my best to schedule outings with friends. Honestly, I need activities to look forward to that don't involve a hospital waiting room, needles, or sleeping.

I still have hairs all over my head, but man oh man are they sparse! They almost don't offer any

---

[9] To learn more about my neuropathy sensations and other potential side effects visit https://chemocare.com/chemotherapy/side-effects/numbness-tingling.aspx for details.

color anymore, and I might give myself another haircut since, at this point, they're just looking silly. Most people familiar with the effects of chemo-related hair loss are always complimenting me on my regrowth, to which I kindly explain that they are still the originals holding on for dear life. I'm happy to report that my eyebrows and eyelashes are still solidly representing and haven't required any "stand-ins" yet. Sadly, however, I have identified three shining silver hairs on my head; before this adventure, I could only ever identify one.

Recently, I've been thinking a lot about capturing a portrait of me stripped down; no, I don't mean naked. Simply no jewelry, no fashionable threads, no busy background, just me. When it came time for the photo session, to avoid looking too pale (much like Casper) and too "sick," I did opt to wear makeup. As luck would have it, my dear friend Tom happened to be on another shoot and had time for me to swing by for a mini portrait session. I wanted to capture the port on my chest since it will be a constant reminder for the next eighteen or more months of this adventure. We took only five pictures, and the first one was the keeper. Not only did the dramatic lighting truly showcase the port, just as I had envisioned, it also captured me.

I won't be absent from CaringBridge this long again; I need to write as much as you long for updates.

Happy first day of fall.

Penny "Good Enough" Casselman

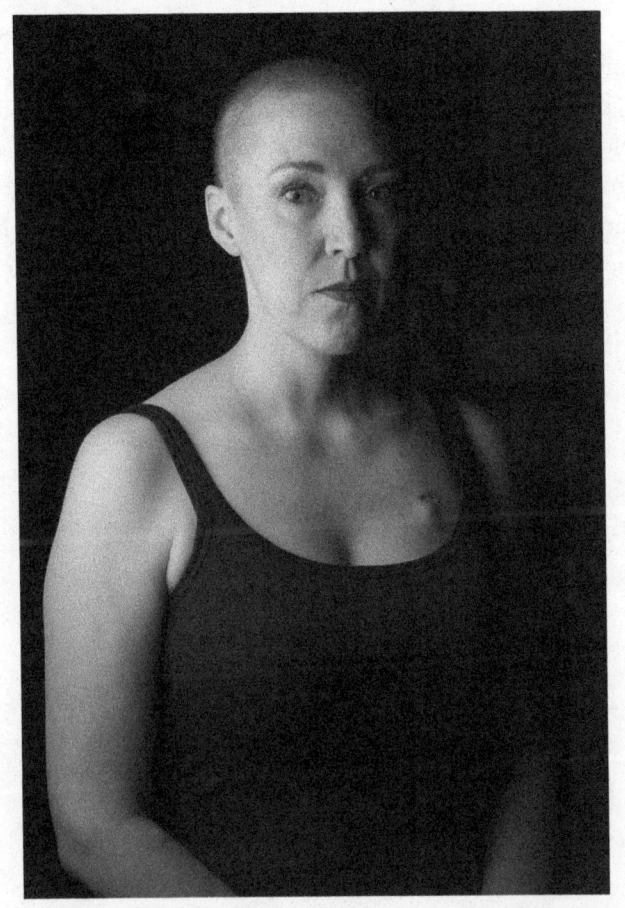

Image provided courtesy of Tom J. Noe Photography

Thinking back to the portrait day, I wish I would have captured the same image but with me smiling. When I look at that picture, I think, "Geez. I look so serious and intense—I was hardly like that *ever* if you had stumbled across me during any portion of my adventure." The image reminds me of the old-timey photos where no one would smile—for apparent reasons, they couldn't. *But* I always imagine them laughing and tearing up after someone told a joke at the conclusion of the sitting. Smiling makes you happy. Smiling makes others happy. Seeing a smiling picture makes me think of every good time I had. They say you can't appreciate sunny days without having experienced gray ones. And you can't enjoy happiness without experiencing sadness. The picture I have immortalized is one that will always have me thinking of the pensive times, the tired days, the surgery preps, recovery weeks, the losses I've endured, and the overwhelm I've experienced. But those support the sparkling days I now create and enjoy, the deepened friendships I've forged, and the optimism I've embraced for the balance of my one sweet life.

Mini Milestone Monday

Sunday, October 1, 2017

Tomorrow is my last day of "double-duty." It's the last day I'll receive both a chemo and Herceptin infusion on the same visit, *ever*!

Yes, I'm putting that thought out into the universe that I will *never* have to go through this oh-so-amazing process again, like EVER. Thoughts become things!

Everything else in my world is status quo.

Not feeling inspired tonight—so this update is succinct.

Happy October.

xo

Penny "Thinking Good Thoughts" Casselman

Second and Ten

Sunday, October 8, 2017

If only the Browns could be as persistent and resilient as me! (Hee hee.)

Only *two* chemo infusions remain . . . a whopping *ten* already under my belt. *Whoa!*

I remember hitting the midway point in pursuing my MBA, ages ago, like, in the '90s. I was exhausted, slightly burned out, hoping the debt I was accruing was going to pay off; I remember giving myself a pep talk to stay the course. You see, I started getting my MBA because I was bored. When I graduated from CWRU, I swore that sixteen solid years in school was enough for any sane person. However, as I sat thoughtfully considering all options, I embraced the following: time was going to pass whether I remained in the program or not. Did I want the remaining one and a half years to pass without meaningful accomplishment, or did I push on at the same pace and just go for it? I went for it. I reflected that during the first half of my pursuit, I managed to keep it all in check, albeit tough at times, knowing that the end would justify the means. I had made it this far and knew I had it in me to finish those few remaining credits for graduation, and I did with flying colors.

Although under entirely different circumstances, I now find it necessary to give myself a similar pep talk.

My knuckles are dragging. I'm tired of chemo, for numerous reasons. I want myself back. Two weeks. Just Two. More. Weeks. I know I can do it, I've come this far, dammit. And if you know of my competitive streak, I *hate* to lose. So, win I will!

Moving on.

Without a mirror in front of me, I sometimes forget. I forget that my head catches the light and casts a shine. I forget that, to others, I don't look like the expected "normal" woman.

I forget that there's a worldwide network of people in this "club" I've become a member of without personal consideration of membership, review of the perks, or acknowledgment of the supposed responsibility I have.

I forget that people make instant judgments about me; they did before too, but they now feel I'm more approachable and can share their thoughts freely with me.

I forget that the "old" Penny will be back; that behind the neuropathy, tiredness, loss of hair, lack of focus, and feeling like I've accomplished nothing in ten weeks, is still the strong, driven, feisty, funny, energetic, athletic, and sassy woman lurking and waiting to take back control and kick some ass.

Lest you think I'm cynical, sad, or depressed: I've still got hairs all over my head. Having said this, however, they are so few and far between that my scalp to hair ratio has now flipped, hence my newfound shine. Honestly, I do forget that, to others, I don't look like the Penny of twelve weeks ago. In essence, I still think, move, and function the same, so from my perspective, I can't really tell a difference. Unless, of course, I'm standing in front of a mirror.

Honestly, ten weeks is *A. Long. Time.* Especially when you're talking chemo. Most people can't stick to a diet, their new year's resolutions, a dream they have, or an exercise routine for ten weeks. Guilty as charged. But I've realized this: if I can drag my tired butt out of bed *every single Monday morning*; drive to the hospital; get vitals taken, blood drawn, and chemo administered; and do it all over again for twelve weeks in a row, I CAN DO ANYTHING! *Bam!*

I find it so odd that my "condition," that people assume based solely on the observation of my hair loss, makes me suddenly more approachable; it's a strange phenomenon. Here are two random encounters I had this past week that illustrate this point.

Thursday, the first night of post-season Indian's baseball playoff action, I had a ticket to the game! Go Windians! A friend mentioned, just hours before the first pitch, that the game was deemed a "red out." I panicked! I don't own anything red! I know, right? I couldn't believe it either! I suddenly found myself in official "scurry mode" to shop and secure something, anything red!

Ten minutes after walking through the doors of a nearby store to start my frantic hunt I heard a soft "ma'am." With the store nearly empty and being focused on my goal, I didn't think twice that the "ma'am" was for me; besides, I'm not old enough to be a ma'am! Upon the second, more audible "ma'am," I turned to look, and sure enough, a woman locked her gaze with mine and made a beeline in my direction. I paused to see how I might help her.

She immediately started sharing her thoughts. "I saw you walk in the store, and I thought to myself, 'I have to walk over.' I have to tell you . . . You look *good*. I mean, I'm not sure the circumstance for your hair, but your face, your head, your whole face just pops. You have such a good shaped head, and your eyebrows and your smile, you look great!" She paused. "Are you a survivor?" That was a lot to launch at me all at once.

I told her I wasn't, yet, but that I had two more treatments and then *yes*, most definitely, I would consider myself a survivor. I then asked her if she was a survivor, and she responded, "No, but I know people who are." She gave me a big hug, reminded me again how amazing I looked, said I should keep the haircut, and she wished for me every good thing. She then went about her own shopping business.

Just a few short hours later, donning my sparkly Indians baseball cap and sporting my newly acquired red anorak—score!—I was making my way through the stadium concourse, along with forty thousand other Indians fans, to find my seat for the game. Suddenly, I felt this "poke" in the middle of my back. Turning to see what friend had spotted me in the masses, I was surprised to see it was no one I knew, just a woman, also wearing a baseball hat. As she passed by me, she lifted up her baseball cap and said, "Nice haircut!" and kept on walking. Yes, she was bald, and if my spidey senses were correct, she, too, was going through her own breast cancer adventure. I'll never know, since our encounter was brief, and like salmon running upstream, she disappeared from my sight as fast as she came into view.

I'm grateful for the people that stop to chat, share a story, or wish me well; it's far better than any alternative I can think of. These interactions also reinforce the knowledge that there are a lot of good people, positive energy, and compassion in this world. I embrace that people, inherently, are good.

Make this week amazing—you get *one life*, so live it to the fullest!

xo

Penny "Like No Other" Casselman

Hot Mess, By the Numbers

Sunday, October 15, 2017

    12,873—Times I've blown my nose in the past month.

    5,742—Times I coughed to clear congestion in the past week.

    100.2—Highest temp I've registered in the last seventy-two hours.

    2.7—Boxes of tissue I retired last week.

    1.85—Days spent in bed this weekend.

    1—Chemo infusion remaining.

    0—Showers I have taken in the past forty-eight hours.

    I am a hot mess right now. I might smell like a hot mess too; however, my sniffer is quite useless, so I can neither confirm nor deny this statement.

    Seriously?! I make it through eleven weeks of chemo, ELEVEN (ironic that I slightly resemble this character, of the same name, from *Stranger Things*; I digress) relatively healthy, then this. Stupid fall allergies majorly compounded by my weak immune system and I have had a weekend of roller coaster temperatures. *Phooey!* You see, being a current chemo patient, if my temperature reaches 100.4, I'm to immediately find the nearest ER. Fingers crossed I'm out of the woods; the last few hours have my temperature falling back within normal ranges.

I am sending positive vibes out to the universe that this fever mumbo jumbo hasn't impacted my blood counts and that tomorrow's lab results are well within the accepted limits for my final—yes I said it, final—chemo to occur. I don't have time for delays, dang it! I've got things to do, people to see, wine to drink, sparkly necklaces to purchase, and fun fall activities to partake in. Thank you very much.

I'll certainly be making another post tomorrow so that you know if chemo is a "go."

Stay tuned.

Penny "I'm So Ready for This Segment of the Adventure to be Over I Can Hardly Stand It" Casselman

Game ON!

Monday, October 16, 2017
Last chemo EVER, commencing!
xoxo
Penny "Kickin' Ass" Casselman

Chemo, chemo, chemo. What can I say but good riddance! The first half of you, not so bad. The last half, a Long. Slow. Slog. Looking back, the one thing I would have loved to have? Noise cancelling headphones. The incessant beeps, chatter of nurses, televisions too loud, and patients piping up asking for a myriad of items, and you can get overstimulated pretty quickly. For me, I always blocked out six hours at the hospital on those days. Having a set of those headphones would have provided me with serene moments of silence and escape.

A few times I took activities to occupy my time, but I never made any headway with them. After a few weeks, I decided my chemo days were for cozying up with my blanket, maybe watching a few episodes of a show on Netflix, and most importantly, napping as long as my body could manage in the heavy, oversized, and stiff chair. The drugs made me too tired for anything that required attention grabbing details.

Lastly, anything I could bring to make my half-day stay more tolerable, I did. My own water bottle, pillow, blanket, fuzzy socks, and snacks were far superior to those same items found at the hospital. And the bonus? I didn't have to ask a nurse to get me anything as I already had my own at the ready.

PART FOUR

Now for My Next Phase

Our Unique Paths

Sadly, I did lose some friends along the way. Not so much by a stated declaration of ending a friendship, but rather a parting of ways as I went down a path different from theirs. At first, I was pissed—not gonna lie. I thought, "Seriously? I get diagnosed with cancer, and all I hear are crickets? No emails of support? Calls to check in? No cards dropped in the mail?" It took me weeks of just sitting with my disappointment before I had my revelation. Truth? I have no idea why they were no longer in my life. None. Zero. Zip. Maybe they had a close family member die of cancer and couldn't fathom watching a friend go through a similar diagnosis. Perhaps they did care but were at a complete and total loss as to what to say or how to act. I was never going to guess what catalyst spawned their departure. So rather than waste time being frustrated and trying to come up with reasons why they ghosted me, I removed myself from the equation, silently forgave them, and wished them well as they continued on their own life's path. Not everyone is meant to be in our life forever. Heck, I've got quite a list myself of people who have come and gone throughout the years. But for one reason or another, the things we had to share or learn from each other had come to an end—and so down our unique paths we'd go.

Wait! Was Yesterday Monday?!

Tuesday, October 24, 2017

First, let's take a pause and do a little dance; not a big dance, just a little one. We need to celebrate the end of my chemo! That part of my adventure is done, *terminé* (French), *erledigt* (German), *fatto* (Italian), *hecho* (Spanish), D. O. N. E. (English). Having said this, however, I'm back at the Cancer Care Center today, donning an ID bracelet, sitting in my seat near the window, waiting to be called back for Herceptin. Cruel timing that the week after I finish chemo, my Herceptin schedule has me back at the main campus.

What makes coming back here more bearable for the next year, at least, are the friendly and beautiful faces of Tierra and Teisha who greet me each week upon arrival. I can't help but smile and feel happy to be here as they check me in. My "normally" scheduled day is Monday, so, technically, I did get a one-day reprieve from coming back here; it's all about gratitude, right? So yes, I'm thankful that yesterday I got to sleep in and not "report for duty" as I had for the previous twelve Mondays. Ok, there was that ONE other time on Labor Day—details, details.

When I walked in today, I was hard to miss. While checking in, Teisha was pushing a patient in a wheelchair, and upon spotting me, she stopped her walk, stepped out from behind the wheelchair, and said, "Wait, Penny, *those shoes*! Girl, I need those shoes! You always have the best shoes and outfit. You got it going *on*!" Of course, Tierra and other medical staff milling around behind the desk also needed to see the shoes. I quickly made an appearance behind the desk and struck a pose or two to showcase my kicks, to which Teisha said, "Work it, girl!" As you can imagine, the commotion I elicited caused everyone in the open-concept and adjacent waiting area to turn and look my way; what are ya' going to do?! Embrace it, I tell ya'!

Since today wasn't Monday, all the faces looking at me from the waiting area were new, to me anyway. After making my entrance, I flashed a big smile and made my way to a posh seat next to the window to wait for my turn to go back for treatment. During my short walk, I met a new "friend," Henry. An older African American man with a smile that lights up a room. We briefly chatted; he said he liked my shoes too, and I said if his smile was any indication of success that he was well on the road to a full recovery.

Today I'm getting a glimpse of my "phase 2" in this adventure; so far, not much is different. What is different? I can drive myself to and from appointments without any issues, so I'm flying solo today. Another difference is I don't require a pre-draw of blood, and because of that, I don't have to subsequently wait for the lab to return results before receiving my infusion. I appreciate this new efficiency.

Cooler temps are here, and with them, my constant need to wear a hat; it's cold dang it! This weekend I had a little chat with my head and told the hairs still representing they needed to tell their neighbors and friends it was safe to come back out, *like seriously*! Come on, guys, I know you can do it! Patience has never been a strong suit of mine, always a work in progress!

I got to thinking, "What are some other things you might be wondering about?" So, here's an attempt to provide you with some insight and updates I may have overlooked or failed to mention in previous posts.

Q: Do you still have your eyebrows and eyelashes?

A: *Yes*, for the most part. I'm having to use my eyebrow gel (finally, my little jar of color was starting to feel lonely) to fill-in and give them a little more substantial look, but all in all they are biologically mine. I still have some practice to do as most days I fill them in and think I've made them uneven. But, hey, I get plenty of compliments on them when I'm out and about, so I can't be doing as bad as I imagine. Eyelashes are still lookin' good.

Q: What about the hair on your legs?

A: I haven't shaved in over a month—woo-hoo! I suppose there had to be *one* good thing to come out of enduring chemo; well, there's that whole eradicating cancer thing too.

Q: Will you receive radiation?

A: Nope! Since I'm having a bilateral mastectomy with reconstruction, I get to skip this process. Why? Long story short, radiation is very damaging to the consistency of breast tissue, making it much more difficult for the surgeon to remove during the mastectomy process. So, since the breast tissue will be removed anyway, there's no need to damage it in advance of being evicted.

Q: When is your surgery?

A: My preference is sometime in January 2018. On November 9, I have an appointment with Dr. Joseph to talk about the next steps and plan for "phase 3" of my adventure; we'll find out if she grants my request. Stay tuned.

Q: How long until you're feeling 100 percent again?

A: This answer kinda bums me out. Last week, when I met with Dr. Hergenroeder, he said the average person is back to 90 percent energy in about six months. Say what?! I've got things to do, people to see, home improvement projects to complete! *Ugh*. I guess I failed to fully account for the massive amount of damage chemo inflicted on my body and my body's ability to return to its former levels of efficient operation. I don't consider myself an "average" person, heck, I still have fuzzy sprouts all over my head. Although I can tell you I continue to get tired if I try to do too many things in a day, but to be fair, it has only been one week since my last chemo infusion.

Q: Are you excited that you'll have hair again soon?

A: *You bet!* I'm keeping it short when it does grow back, like pixie short! Now that I've discovered my head is a good shape, people like the buzz cut, and the maintenance is, well, a walk in the park, there's no need to have hair as I had before, *ever*! I am excited that I'll have more hairs to provide insulation on top—the sparse representation now is chilly!

Q: How long will your Herceptin infusions continue?

A: I will "report for duty" every third week, through July 2018. Yeah, a cool nine months away. I know this will fly by, but today it feels out of reach.

Q: Are you drinking alcoholic beverages again?

A: *Yes!* Although, I haven't had a drink since concluding chemo. Since I'm sure I'm a lightweight, I thought I should try having my first drink at home to see how I do before throwing back a few with friends while out on the town. After my sinus issues last week, I'm finally starting to feel well enough to toast my milestone. Cheers indeed, my friend!

Q: Are you doing anything to celebrate being done with chemo?

A: H-E-double hockey sticks YES I am! This woman booked a flight to visit my aunt and uncle out in Southern California for two solid weeks in November! Honestly, if all I do is sit on the beach and stare at the ocean, I will consider my trip a success! I need a change of scenery, a change of pace, different walls to look at, and new air to breathe.

Q: Anything else to share?

A: Yes, and this one bummed me out. Last week when I met with Dr. Hergenroeder, he relayed the news that I'll have to take a daily pill for five years after my surgery is complete. For some reason, I thought that having surgery was going to supersede any need for taking daily pills; I was wrong. I was in shock, so I have no idea the name of the medicine, what it's for, or what side effects I might experience. I'll see Dr. Hergenroeder again on November 6 and will ask those questions then. Here I thought I'd have all this behind me in 2018, not so much. The good news? The pill won't require a trip to the hospital, whew, and I'll convince myself that it's only a daily vitamin, so I don't have to think about this adventure Every. Single. Day.

Cheers to phase 1 behind me!

Penny "I'm Ready to Be a Beach Bum" Casselman

The staff—hands down—were the reason I enjoyed going to the Cancer Care Center. Without the interaction with reception, support staff, nurses, and doctors, I might have forgotten how to chat with other humans. I stayed strong, positive, and upbeat when I was around others, but my trek down cancer road was quite lonely. My closest friends all are "desk-dwelling" professionals—like I was once. Because of this, my days spent at home were very quiet and often devoid of any engaging interaction. Having appointments at the hospital gave me a reason to set the alarm, take a shower, get dressed, wear high heels—if for no other reason than "I can"—slap on some makeup, and waltz in somewhere with a smile and a mission. After all, keeping my appointments at the hospital *was* my job—and arguably the most critical role in my life—and I took it very seriously.

The Countdown Begins

Monday, November 6, 2017

Nine days until I'm in Southern California. So much to do, so little time.

It's starting to hit me how long I'll be out of town and all the planning I need to do for this trip in order for it to be the getaway I'm looking for. I've got my planner at the ready and checkmarks are being ticked off the lengthy to-do list in steady succession; it's all coming into focus!

Last week was my first week with nada, none, absolutely ZERO visits to a doctor's exam room or hospital setting, woo-hoo! This week, however, I'm back at it with a visit to Dr. Joseph to discuss phase 2 of this hair-raising adventure; I'm too punny, ha! The following week, just days before I leave on my vaca, I'll be back at the hospital for a Herceptin infusion. Then *yes*, I have three weeks clear of appointments, procedures, or other medical obligations on the calendar; *three whole weeks*! This girl is grinning ear to ear!

I'm ready to have hair! I look good in hats, thank goodness, but in the past, they've always been optional, not mandatory; I'm so ready to have the option again! For the hairs that have hung on for dear life and continue to grow, a hair trim is needed before jet-setting across the country. I'm still waiting to see signs of new life sprouting on the noggin; however, it's still just the trusty holdouts representing; soon enough they'll be joined by others, I know.

My Christmas shopping is almost done, hooray! Typically, I'm done shopping by September, so this year I've had a tad bit of self-imposed stress with it being November and finding myself with gifts still to be purchased. Fear not, I have plans to have all gifts purchased in advance of my departure. The wrapping can wait until I return; I'm ambitious, but not that ambitious.

I know my energy is returning as I no longer find it necessary to take a nap every single day; I do love my naps, though. I'm sure my blood counts still have some rebounding to do before they are considered within normal ranges, but it's so lovely to feel spunky again!

Cheers to another *holi-daze* right around the corner!

Kisses to you.

Penny "Santa's *Best* Little Helper" Casselman

Phase Two

Friday, November 10, 2017

Yesterday I met with Dr. Joseph for a post-chemo recap, general exam, and to chat about the next steps in preparation for my surgeries.

Given my previous conversation with Dr. Hergenroeder and since my surgeries were more or less optional, I could wait for any duration of time before proceeding. Therefore, I was slightly taken back when, at first, Dr. Joseph didn't ask when I wanted the surgery and instead started talking about scheduling it for early December. *Whoa Nelly!* This woman isn't prepared for such a whirlwind of activity before the close of 2017. That's like one month away!

Calmly taking a deep breath, I looked at her and pleaded my case that "I'd like to wait until after the holidays so I can enjoy them without pain or discomfort and just, well, relax, laugh, imbibe, and chill." After Dr. Joseph audibly ran through my case and acknowledged the already executed series of surgeries and infusions. She weighed the complexity of my upcoming procedures, the risk factors associated with someone of my unique circumstances, the need for me to still schedule appointments to regroup with the other two surgeons for their game plan, and the fact I'll be in California beginning next week through November 30 (that's just five days away, you knew I had to reference that somewhere in here!) and she relented and said she was "ok" with waiting until January. *Yay!*

I have no doubt Dr. Joseph will move to coordinate my three-surgeon high-five-tag-you're-it triple surgery the first week of the year. Nothing like starting 2018 off with a big bang, I mean big boobs, wait, just boobs, but new boobs. Did I say boobs enough? *Ha!*

I attend yoga every Saturday morning and am surrounded by people all having some connection to cancer, whether that's through their own experience or someone close to them. As you can imagine, I see many of the same people week after week, and I've made a few lovely acquaintances along the way. One such friendly face is Beth, a tall thin woman sporting a full head of blonde hair. One day after class, she was asking me how my treatments were going and how I was feeling. I filled her in and then asked what her circumstances had been and how she was navigating everything.

Here's where perspective is everything. You just never know what someone else is going through only by looking at them.

Beth, during the process of eliminating her cancer, had to have a lung removed. *A lung!* Suddenly, I felt silly that I was just going to lose my boobs and ovaries, neither of which I need to live. Let me say that again; she is missing a *lung*. Beth does yoga to help strengthen her muscles and stretch her rib cage. You see, she has a cavern where her lung was—there is no filling in of a missing lung—and, in turn, her ribs want to collapse. *She is amazing* and continues to persevere. I got nothin' on her.

I'm not an organized group person. I didn't join a sorority in college, and once I was unleashed in the real world, I tried the Junior League, resulting in an epic fail. So, when I heard of a cancer support group, I rolled my eyes. I thought, "The last place I want to be is somewhere that I'm surrounded by a bunch of people going through cancer." Surprisingly, it was exactly what I needed. Although I was happy to talk all things cancer with friends and family, I knew they couldn't fully *"get it"* unless they went through it. The people at the Gathering Place, they got it. Going through cancer treatment, it's rare that someone asks you for insight; usually you're the one asking doctors and nurses for information. So, finding a support group made me feel useful, and I was thankful for real people talk and new perspectives on surgeries, healing, body image, and a whole host of other topics that aren't normal discourse in society.

> I've come a long way from where I was just a few short months ago, although I believe my progression is like most any other coming-to-terms type of event.
>
> They're just boobs.
>
> They're just ovaries.
>
> I am thankful those are the only bits and pieces I'm saying goodbye to.
>
> Boobs can be recreated and will be. Ovaries only have a certain shelf life anyway and, given

time, would fail on me sooner than later, so I'm just steppin' up and making the decision for them as to when they cease to function.

Years ago, I had toyed with the idea of donating my body to science—after I died, of course—for medical students to use when learning anatomy. I think that's entirely off the table at this point. I can just see it now.

Med student: <raises hand> Professor, mine's missing her gallbladder.

Prof: Ok, please join another group to inspect their cadaver's gallbladder.

-Thirty minutes later-

Med student: <raises a hand, again> Um, Professor, mine's also missing her mammary glands.

Prof: Ok, once again, please join another group to inspect these organs.

-Forty-five minutes later-

Med student: <agitated, raises hand yet again> Professor, this is getting ridiculous, seriously, mine's also missing her ovaries.

Prof: Ok, ok. We'll send her off to the crime scene folks to use in their investigative models. Please join another group for the duration of this semester.

Med student: *Thank goodness!*

I crack myself up.

I know I'll survive the upcoming events and do it with style, grace, and gratitude. What else is there, right?

Until my next update, stay safe.

Penny "Lead Investigator, CSI: Cleveland" Casselman

And, They're Off!

Saturday, November 25, 2017

I thought I was prepared.

I thought they had shared everything with me.

I thought the part of "looking like a cancer patient" was behind me.

A good friend of mine had mentioned that one of her friends (a male) said he didn't lose his eyebrows until after his chemo was complete. At the time, I was nearly at the end of my infusions and thought to myself, "I've made it this far maintaining sparse hairs all over my head, all my eyebrows, and all my eyelashes, why would she share this with me? I'm an outlier; I'll be fine." Not so much. Two days ago, my eyebrows said, "Peace out!" And, not to be outdone, my eyelashes said, "Oh, yeah? Watch this!"—insert mic drop—and they left too.

Unlike my hair sprouts that lingered, my brows and lashes were completely gone in a matter of forty-eight hours; a timeframe I wasn't quite prepared to deal with, especially this late in the adventure. Every day, we all lose hairs, which are immediately replaced with new growth. I had anticipated this natural attrition would leave me a little light since nothing new would resurface until chemo had concluded. Shh, don't tell, but I had been filling in my brows for a few weeks. When preparing for my trip, I naturally packed my eyebrow gel and brush, but, unfortunately, I chose to leave behind my faux eyelashes as I had assumed, incorrectly, that I wouldn't need them. At least I squeezed in a few weeks of "connecting the dots" above my eyes before needing to freehand the brows in; a process that, for a type-A person like me, is difficult as they are never *exactly* even and take a little longer than I would care to spend during my usual morning routine.

Luckily, I don't have anyone to impress while on vacation. My aunt said I look cute, and I told her she had to say that because she was my aunt. Right now, I think I look like one of those hairless cats—weird, wiry things.

Honestly, my eyebrows are already growing back. The new growth is nothing more than blonde fuzz, so recreating them each morning is a must. I think the old sprouts were kicked out to make room for the new. Eyelashes show no signs, yet, of new life.

My vacation is rounding its final stretch, and as Cleveland looms closer, I'm wondering why I live somewhere that gets so cold and gray? A beach, ocean, and palms make for a beautiful Thanksgiving backdrop!

Given this week was Thanksgiving, here are just a few of the things I'm thankful for:

YOU
Modern medicine
Functioning hair follicles
Airplanes
People who smile
Holiday cheer
Stretching
Laughing
And last, but not least, alcoholic beverages

Here's lookin' at you, kid!
Penny "Gobble Gobble" Casselman

California was exactly what I needed. I wanted to forget I was different, that something was wrong with me. I wanted—no needed—to feel like it was all over. The sound of the ocean rushing to the shore, yoga on the daily, sunshine on my skin, and a delicious home-cooked Thanksgiving meal were what my body and soul needed to recharge in preparation for the second part of my adventure.

Doctors and nurses can tell you at length what to expect when going through chemo, but until you experience it, you don't fully know all the nuances and exactly how your body will react. Act two was on the horizon for me. I had talked to every surgeon and knew what to expect, but I wasn't sure how I was going to process everything—both physically and mentally. So, when it came time for me to say goodbye, it was a lot to process. I got back to Cleveland and found myself smack dab back in the middle of everything—nothing had changed. I looked at my calendar to see just four days after returning I'd be back at the hospital for an appointment and an infusion. It was evident that the adventure for me was far from over. And I'd be back on the hamster wheel soon enough.

Back to Reality

Thursday, December 7, 2017

Southern California was just what this girl needed. Walks along the beach Every. Single. Day. The weight I had lost during chemo was replaced in short order after eating and drinking my way through new restaurants, slipping into a food coma after Thanksgiving, enjoying daily social hour before happy hour,[10] and finally, finishing each evening with a nightcap chillin' with my aunt and uncle. Indeed, so much to be thankful for this year, despite the obvious speedbump.

I'm finally back on Cleveland time, but it wasn't easy, the coming back or the time change shift. But as you already know, I persevere.

Within forty-eight hours of touching down, I was in a car headed back to Fort Wayne, Indiana, to attend my extended family Christmas gathering. It was a whirlwind of a week, for sure.

My mom's mom is still alive. She's alert, living on her own, and is ninety-one. When this

---

[10] Social hour, for those of you not in the know, is the cocktail hour which immediately precedes happy hour. You're welcome. Cheers!

adventure kicked off, I had asked my aunts and uncle not to share with her what I was going through. My grandma had already buried her eldest daughter, something no mother should ever have to do, and I didn't want her to worry about me now succumbing to the very start of events that took her daughter so many years ago. I had every intention of telling her *after* I was through everything and thriving. It wasn't until everyone started to arrive for the Christmas festivities that my eyes got wide as saucers when I heard my cousin yell, "Grandma's here." I started the frantic inquiry with each aunt and my uncle, silently mouthing to each, "Did you tell Grandma yet?" and back from each came a head shake and a silent "No." I shouldn't have been surprised, they did exactly what I had asked them to do.

I kept myself out of her sight until I had composed my thoughts. I mean, how can you tell your grandma you're dealing with the same disease that took her daughter and, oh by the way, it was Mom who passed it on to me? *Ugh.* In short order I had my plan, thank goodness I think quickly on my feet. I made my way to the room she was in, and as I rounded the corner, she spotted me, took in a long gaze, and then said, "What'd you do that for?!" I cracked up as she was referring to my sparse buzz cut, I had to smile.

I responded with, "Well, Grandma, that's an interesting story, let's go have a seat in the living room. How are you?" She took the news well, with obvious concern. I know it was good for her to see me laughing, smiling, talking, eating, doing all the normal things people do, and, other than the sparse hair, looking and acting healthy.

Anyway, back to the present. I wanted to wait and write again until I had a surgery date, and today that news came. The eviction of the "no good, freeloading lady parts" will occur on the same day as the first stages of reconstruction for the "yes they're fake, the first ones tried to kill me." That day is Wednesday, January 24.

I'm not sure how I feel about having this scheduled. It's later than I had planned but, now that it's an actual date on my calendar, it seems too soon. There's never a good time for anything, I suppose. You just jump in, feet first, hoping that all well-laid plans are in place, details reviewed, and a little universal goodwill is at your back to carry you through.

Here's a few illustrations of never a good time: First, shortly after I purchased my very first new car, negotiated all by myself, I lost my job. Second, after I bought the house I currently live in, the housing market collapsed.

Having laid those at your feet, here are some illustrations of universal goodwill carrying me through: First, after deciding to go back to school for my MBA, I was unwittingly put in the path of connecting with two of my closest friends, then just strangers. Second, once, after waiting in line for twenty-five minutes to get my car washed, I let someone cut in line before me. This poor woman had been waiting to enter the same line from the other direction of traffic flow and no one had budged; I figured what was one more car length for me to wait. Imagine my surprise when

I finally got up to pay for my car wash, and the attendant said I owed nothing; the person in front of me paid for mine.

Every single event was the right thing to do at the time, given the information I had at hand. Even those unfortunate events now give me perspective, and I wouldn't be the person I am today without those experiences. So, I look at this date, Wednesday, January 24, and know it's the perfect date I need to accomplish the outcome I want—*perfect boobs*! I jest, I jest. I wanted to make sure you're still with me here. Besides the perfect boobs, I said it again, hee hee, I'll have a *long*, *happy*, and *healthy* life ahead of me.

My sprouts are returning everywhere! I noticed today I had little sprouts popping up on the back of my hand, say *what*?! I swear, the next time you see me, if I look like a werewolf girl, you're allowed to walk right by me and pretend you didn't see me. *Ha!* Seriously though—new hair growth on my hands? Side note, the hairs are very blonde and not detectible by a casual glance, whew! My brows are getting easier to fill in as a very faint outline is starting to appear. Eyelashes are still about a millimeter long; pull out a ruler and look at how short that is, holy moly! The last hairy thought I'll share is this: You know how as a baby's hair starts to grow, they get that "bald ring" from where their head rests on the bed or in their car seat? Please, please, please, for the love of all things sacred, let my hair grow in evenly!

Switching gears. While in California, my aunt shared with me this "thing" that's sweeping through cities across the US. Residents take small rocks, paint them, and then sprinkle them conspicuously around town for an unsuspecting passerby to find. I liken it to urban trail magic. The spotter is encouraged to pick up the rock and relocate it in hopes of passing along the joy of discovery to another passerby. Or, if they found a connection with the message or image on the rock, keep it as a joyful reminder of their find and a frequent reminder of the sentiment. As I was headed home after one of my last morning walks along the beach, I rounded a turn when I spotted a rock near the downspout of a garage gutter. It was dated 11/28/17, which was cool since I was in town when it was created, and after reading the message, I knew it was meant for me. It now sits on my desk as a reminder of the remaining adventure I have yet to experience. The message painted with colorful dotted flair reads No Bad Days. Indeed, a statement I can get behind.

With much love, gratitude, and holiday cheer to you.

Penny "the Human Embodiment of the Chia Pet Phenomenon" Casselman

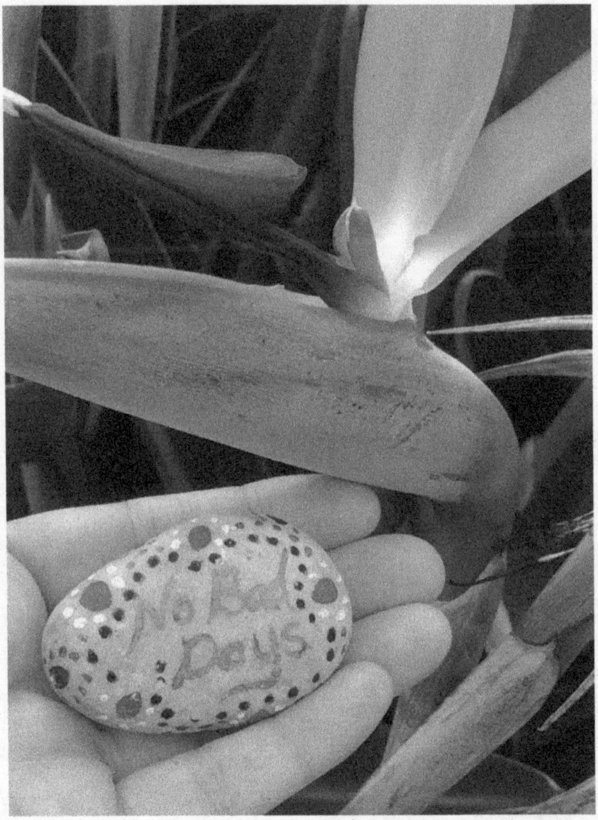
No Bad
Days

Dear Santa

Monday, December 25, 2017

Dear Santa,

Merry Christmas!

If you had told me a year ago, I'd be excited about asking for hair, eyelashes, and eyebrows for Christmas gifts I would have said, "What say? Come again?" Yet here I sit so thankful that you, and the work of your smallest elven helpers (follicles), made this girl's Christmas wish come true! Although I'm still drawing on eyebrows, the process is taking less time as the outline of where they should be is nearly complete. My eyelashes can now support mascara, albeit a single swipe, but it gives my irises a little more dramatic frame for their daily sparkling performances. My noggin is nearly completely wrapped with dark, fuzzy hair and will soon be so happy to give up its shining feature as it prefers to let my personality have that distinction.

Speaking of hair, you and your cohort in crime (a.k.a. the Universe) sure do know how to surprise me with gifts! You must have heard the thoughts tumbling in my head about who cuts my hair now. I would have never thought that while helping a friend in her gallery during the holidays, I'd get a compliment from a woman about my hair; low and behold she's a barber! To top that off, she works at a barbershop so close to where I live I can walk there in the summer; I suppose I could walk there in the winter too, but I'm not as keen on the weather conditions this time of year. She said I could swing by for a complimentary Christmas cut, so last week, I stopped in, plopped down in her chair, and got a sweet little tune-up for my sprouts! I was the only woman in a chair; the other women were working behind them. This may sound silly, but, Santa, I'm so glad you put her directly in my path as I have a new friend and a highly skilled barber to help keep me looking fierce into 2018.

Your other cohort in crime (a.k.a. Mother Nature) did an excellent job providing a white Christmas; not too much, but enough to cover everything in a blanket of sparkling white. Please feel free to take it back tomorrow and save it for this time next year; a girl can wish, right?

You know, Santa, we have a lot in common—I love me some good Christmas tunes, we both have a dependable sleigh—side note, I wish mine ran on carrots—and we *love* to give gifts. And when I say *love* to give gifts, you know I mean LOVE TO GIVE GIFTS! I don't think of it as a sickness, although some would argue that, but like the Grinch, giving makes my heart grow three sizes bigger. I've already celebrated Christmas five times and still have about four to go; my heart might just leap out of my chest!

Thanks, too, for giving all my nurses and doctors the day off today; they deserve it! I'll see them all tomorrow as I head back to the hospital for another dose of Herceptin, and so my adventure continues. Can't wait to hear how you surprised them too!

Keep up the excellent work, Santa, thanks for keeping me in your thoughts and delivering such amazing gifts this year! Best. Christmas. Ever.

With a big heart full of health, happiness, and hope,

Penny "Rudolph" Casselman

Congratulations!

Tuesday, January 2, 2018
　Dear Baby New Year,
　So excited to welcome you to the world! I can't believe you've finally arrived.
　Since Santa received a letter from me, I thought it only fitting that you should receive one too.
　Back in May, I wasn't even thinking of you yet; I was all consumed with your brother, Mr. 2017, and you were but a glimmer in my eye. Then along came June, like a freight train out of nowhere, and I couldn't wait for you to get here. Unfortunately, however, just the thought of you filled me with a melancholy I hadn't felt before. At times, those thoughts were heavy and overwhelming but, luckily, other times, nothing more than a light breeze through my mind. I hated to wish for time to pass more quickly in hopes of hastening your arrival. This life is too short under normal circumstances, but, at the time, you seemed a lifetime away, and I was growing weary. And now, so suddenly you're here—just like that.

Now that your brother is out of the picture, I get asked frequently what I learned from him. Although I do have a growing list, I'm not sure I'm quite ready to share, yet, as I know my adventure is far from over and, like him, you'll provide me insights too. And so, I patiently wait for the lessons and learnings to commence.

Although it's only been two days since your arrival, you've already ushered forth a pep in my step. Thank you. Thank you. Thank you! I'm feeling much more back to my sassy self, and although she's leaving again on January 24, she'll be back just a few short months later and, as always, will be welcomed with open arms, a sparkling smile, and a heart full of gratitude.

Like Santa, you and I also have several traits in common. We both like bottles, although mine usually contains bubbling contents. We're both fierce optimists, whether by design or necessity. We look forward to growing, you in stature, and me in cognitive pursuits. We stare in wide-eyed wonder at the world around us, always giddy with what we discover. We stay grounded knowing we could not, under any circumstance, navigate this adventure alone as we're both still newbies to this whole thing.

I'm anxious to see what unfolds during your tenure. I know you're going to grow up too fast and, just like your brother before you, disappear in the blink of an eye. Please stay in touch; somehow, I know we're both going to slay 2018!

Cheers!

Penny "Brrr, Where is Heat Miser When You Need Him?" Casselman

PART FIVE

Surgery Round One

Live in the Moment

My hair was starting to grow back, my energy was returning, and I was beginning to feel back to normal. I bought a new dress and made plans to hit the town on New Year's Eve. Being surrounded by friends and a festive atmosphere at every turn was just what this girl needed. But I knew it was short-lived.

My mantra for the balance of January was live in the moment, it's all you've got. It never felt like my adventure was over. Chemo was only a temporary stop on my trip, and one of the least invasive procedures I'd have. Other than taking my hair and disrupting my sleep and energy, it wasn't that bad. I knew my hair would grow back, my sleep would normalize, and my energy would return. In the next phase, however, everything about my body would change, forever; and I had no idea how I would react. Although I was given all the textbook knowledge from my doctors, and heard from other women what they experienced, each person—even if we have the same diagnosis—can react differently to the same drugs. Medicine is both a science and an art.

With my lumpectomy, I retained the hallmark features of a woman—boobs—and I still had ovaries producing estrogen. My next round of procedures would have me physically looking different, chemically processing different, and mentally grappling with the changes that accompany all my losses. I was ready to keep this adventure moving; I could only wonder for so long before I started making myself nuts. I was ready to embrace the new me with boob replacements, even though I knew they'd be nothing like the originals. I was also happy to embrace the popular T-shirt slogan, "Yes they're fake, the real ones tried to kill me." And once the ovaries are evicted, lord help me if I start growing a mustache!

I, Penny

Tuesday, January 23, 2018

It's here.

It's finally here.

No more waiting, thinking, planning, fretting, painting, or shopping can be done, time's up.

Approximately ten days ago, I felt the need to give my office a facelift since, you know, nothing says life-changing-surgery-is-right-around-the-corner like a semi-major room renovation. *Ha!* I figured if I was going to look different, so should something else I have to see nearly every day. Well, that and doing home improvement projects are therapy for me. Something about the solitude, the precision of task, the creative element, and planning to bring it all together; pure bliss. The walls are now the most stunning deep blue—think the clearest sky at midnight or the deepest ocean depth. The trim is a soothing candlelight white, and together with the new drapes my office gives off the coziest of room vibes I've ever assembled. Now that it's all done—I finished putting it all back together again at nine p.m. this evening—I'm in love with the result; it's exactly what I had envisioned and hoped for.

My office now seems like an excellent metaphor for my surgery tomorrow; my body a new landscape with new "colors" to behold. I have every confidence that soon, maybe not tomorrow or next week, I'll be in love with the changes that are about to take place. I'll come out on the other side wiser, stronger, braver, and fiercer than I ever thought I would be but exactly what I had secretly envisioned. Being human, I've had sad moments, for sure, but they are just that, moments. Points in time that roar like a fierce storm and then, as quickly as they came, dissolve into calm as I remind myself, "They're just boobs; they're just ovaries."

I've had the pleasure of meeting and speaking with so many amazing women who have gone before me and are now thriving. I'm reminded daily of the love and support I have from family and friends, and for that, I cannot express enough of my gratitude, good fortune, and love for you.

Switching gears. Allow me to share some FAQs that, I'm sure, have been on your mind.

Q: What time is your surgery?

A: I have to report to the surgical wing at 8:45 a.m. They did not provide a start time for the surgery itself.

Q: How long is your surgery?

A: The expected duration of my time on the operating table is approximately six hours.

Q: What, exactly, are you having done again?

A: I am having a bilateral mastectomy immediately followed by phase 1 of breast reconstruction finishing up with a salpingectomy-oophorectomy. In layman's terms: Boobs are coming off. Faux boobs are starting phase 1. Fallopian tubes and ovaries are being removed.

Q: Do you have a hospital stay?

A: Yes. At least one night and perhaps a second depending upon how the doctors feel my body is handling the post-op recovery.

Q: How many doctors do you have for this surgery?

A: Three. I've joked that this is going to be a tag-team surgery. I envision that each will high five the next as they pass each other outside the door of the OR, exclaiming, "You're up!"

Q: Why three doctors?

A: One to take the boobs off. One to start the new boobs. One to take the fallopian tubes and ovaries out. Honestly, I think it's pretty cool. I have half the medical staff at my beck and call tomorrow!

Q: What can we do to help?

A: Send good vibes, healing thoughts, and peaceful energy my way; I'll take it all!

Q: How long do they anticipate your recovery to take?

A: I've heard about six weeks. This doesn't mean that for the entire six-week duration I'm down for the count, just that it may take six weeks until I have a substantial amount of energy and flexibility and can begin to resume a full menu of activities.

Q: Is this your last surgery?

A: No. I will still need to undergo breast reconstruction—phase 2. This will most likely occur in May. Yay! New boobs for my forty-sixth birthday.

I'm still planning on juicing tonight and enjoying a healthy green drink before my midnight fasting deadline. Lastly, because why not squeeze one more thing into this evening, I still need to shower with my presurgical wash, which will have me smelling like a freshly cleaned toilet bowl. I kid you not, my skin will be a scratch-n-sniff version of Clorox toilet bowl gel.

And with that lovely vision, I bid you goodnight. This girl is tired.

Penny "Triple Doctor" Casselman

After the paint clean up, juicing, and my presurgical shower, it was nearly midnight. I was utterly exhausted, mentally and physically. The minute my head hit the pillow that night, I was out. Since I wasn't allowed to eat or drink the morning of surgery, I lay in bed until thirty minutes before my hospital departure—I only needed time to shower again, dress, and walk out the door. I made sure to plan my outfit appropriately—elastic-waist joggers, a button-up linen shirt, and slip-on shoes. I didn't want to expend any unnecessary energy or go through pretzel-twisting arm movements to get dressed on the other side of surgery since I had no idea how I was going to feel. Although I got to the hospital by 8:30 a.m., they didn't wheel me back until noon. As each hour ticked by, I grew increasingly thirsty and was borderline hangry. I know now I could never compete on *Naked and Afraid*; I wouldn't make it past one full day without food or water.

Surgery flew by, for me, anyway. One minute my eyelids were heavy and starting to close; the next, they were heavy and fighting to open. For everyone else, it clocked in at a tad over five hours. I know it was nerve-wracking for everyone not on the operating table, doctors excluded—they were calm, cool, and collected. My boyfriend, Joe, provided updates to everyone as, one by one, the surgeons came out and gave him an update. Of course, all the reports about how I did were glowing—I didn't expect anything less. I'm a stellar patient, for sure! Even under general anesthesia, my body follows doctors' orders.

Surgery Day Update

Wednesday, January 24, 2018

    Penny is out of surgery and heading to recovery. Each surgeon was extremely positive and said Penny did fantastic. I hope to see her in an hour or so. She got through another significant step in the journey! Thank you for your love and support.

    —Joe

    PS, I'll let Penny take it from here.

I Live!

Thursday, January 25, 2018

This will be brief, as I'm exhausted! And typing to you on my phone from my hospital bed.

It was a rough night, but today I start the recovery process yet again. Details will be forthcoming when I have a real keyboard in front of me and have gotten a little more sleep.

I've been visited by every surgical team this morning, and they're all pleased with the outcome. I believe I'll be discharged later today, stay tuned.

Thank you for all your love and support; it means the world!

Peace, love, and lots of naps to you!

Penny "Pincushion" Casselman

I only remained in the hospital for one night. I wanted to go home, stat. I knew I'd sleep better in my bed. Not to mention I wouldn't have nursing staff checking in on me hourly to ensure my pulse, temperature, and oxygen levels were good. Temperature swipes, a blood pressure cuff, and a finger clamp do not make for a restful sleep.

Home

Thursday, January 25, 2018

Hard to believe that nearly thirty-six hours ago I was undergoing major surgery, and tonight at 9:04 p.m., I'm sitting in my basement watching an episode of *The Americans*, unbelievable.

Modern medicine is nothing short of amazing. I'm so thankful I was born when I was; my mom wasn't so lucky. Tonight, I miss her.

Tomorrow is a new day full of new adventures and, fingers crossed, much more REM sleep for this girl. Until my next post, that'll be composed from the comfort of my newly decorated and oh-so cozy office, good night from Shaker Heights.

xo

Penny "Like Mother Like Daughter" Casselman

This was the first night I really missed my mom. And by miss I mean wished she was still alive. There's not a lot I remember about her; after all, I was quite young. And missing someone whom you're now older than is a little strange. Other than genetics, and some would say appearance, we have little else in common. I have experienced more life than her, never had kids, and experienced radically different approaches to eliminating our cancer. I thought about how easy my adventure had been relative to hers. She took me with her one day to chemo—it may have been more than once, but I don't remember. Anyway, I recall her asking the nurse for a piece of candy. My mom explained that during chemo, it helped keep the metal taste in her mouth at bay.

My surgery seemed so effortless. But I left the hospital with more scars than I went in with. I also left with drains coming out of my body as I began the transition to faux boobs. Looking back on the numerous procedures, infusions, and surgeries that I underwent, the drains were the most challenging, frustrating, cumbersome, annoying, uncomfortable, disruptive, and other-worldly part of my adventure. I wish I could say I'll never see them again, but any faux body part—including hips, shoulders, and yes, even my boobs—isn't made as well as the original and will, at some point in the future, need to be replaced. Sigh. The silver lining is at least I know what to expect the next time around.

Five Days Out

Monday, January 29, 2018

    Five days out and I really can't complain; ok, maybe just a little bit, more on that later. Since so many days have passed since my surgery without a substantial update, let's all hop in the "way back machine" and start again on Tuesday, January 23.

    Strap in, here we go!

    I slept fine the night before surgery, partially because I completely wore myself out with a frantic push to finalize my office makeover. Every time I walk past my office door, I have to stop and admire my work; I know, don't break my arm patting myself on the back. This update is being composed from my IKEA Poang chair in the corner while I gaze upon my dark, mysterious, and magical midnight-blue walls.

    Tuesday evening, I didn't climb into bed until 11:30 p.m. and, even at that late hour, didn't feel I had accomplished enough before surgery, but my body cried uncle so off to bed I went. Wednesday morning came swiftly. Getting ready that morning was a breeze! I couldn't use lotion, wear makeup, or eat, so all I had to do was scrub up in the shower with Clorox gel, throw clothes on, and walk out the door. I had to report to the surgery center at 8:45 a.m., but before that, I needed my port accessed across the street by nurses at the Cancer Care Center; you see nurses need to be trained on how to access a port, and not all are. I planned to arrive at the main campus by 8:15 a.m., a target I hit with ease.

At 9:30 a.m., I was whisked away to surgery prep where all my earthly possessions were taken from me—well, the ones I brought with me, anyway—and placed in a locker until their retrieval and subsequent delivery to my post-surgery hospital room. Then the long, arduous task of waiting commenced, and wait, I did.

One hour.

Two hours.

At this point, I asked the universe to hold in reserve all the energy from those near and far that was pouring in, since—I'm just guessing here—my friends and family thought I was already "under the knife" by the time eleven a.m. rolled around. Instead, I was still staring at a pale-yellow hospital wall huddled under two blankets to keep warm. Although the 3XL hospital gown I was wrapped in provided ample coverage, it did little for retention of body heat.

I'm a girl who no later than one hour after waking will find a piping hot cup of black coffee in her hand and next to me a bowl of my current cereal of choice topped to the brim with soy milk; not the case this day, for a good reason. Dr. Resnick and her team came in for a pre-op chat, all carrying some form of carbonated and caffeinated bottled beverage. I told them I could really go for a swig, to which they quickly grabbed their bottles and hid them from view saying, "Nothing to see here," and smiling. I figured if anyone was going to suffer a slight headache from caffeine withdrawal, it should be me, not the medical staff; caffeine on, I say!

Finally, shortly after 11:30 a.m., the call came for me to be wheeled back to the OR. At the strike of noon, the superstar, tag-team surgery began.

In the blink of an eye, for me anyway, I found myself back in the same pale-yellow room with a few notable modifications. I no longer had fallopian tubes or ovaries. I no longer had breasts—of the biologically grown kind. My bed was facing the opposite direction. And I was alone.

I remained alone for a good hour (insert complaint #1).

The hallway outside my recovery bay was abuzz with activity, just not directed at me. It took me a few minutes to muster the energy to raise my "Hello?!" to a level that could be detected by anyone within earshot, I didn't care who at that point. The first person, seemingly annoyed, asked if I was in pain, I said no, and off they went. WAIT! *Ugh!* I had to start the entire process of gathering the energy to raise my voice over again for some attention. I finally received some recognition by a few people, but I don't fully recall our conversations or the reasoning behind me being alone this long. After what seemed like forever, and through numerous tears of loneliness and frustration, I was finally wheeled to my overnight accommodations. The staff never brought anyone to see me during this immediate post-op time. Although my surgery ended slightly before six p.m., I didn't lay eyes on my three in-person—and very patient—supporters until around eight p.m.

    I was lucky to be given a private room, but there were a few curious caveats. The reason it took so long for me to exit post-op was that they were trying to secure a room for me. They did eventually succeed; however, I was placed on the orthopedic floor in a room that, from the looks of it, was mainly used as a dumping ground for wayward furniture. Immediately after being wheeled in the room, some staffers came to carry out an extra table and a couple random lounge chairs that were just hanging out in the corner. It made the room feel less cluttered, but honestly, those items could have stayed, I didn't care. I had a place to myself which made me very happy. And within minutes of arriving, my three supporters were at my bedside. Their stay was brief as I'm sure you can imagine; I was wiped out. I was also a tad bit thirsty and hungry and decided to eat two saltine crackers and drink a few sips of water before getting ready to pass out. And pass out I did, only to be awakened about ninety minutes later for vitals and a touch base from my overnight staff.

    I've had several surgeries in my life and have experienced no adverse effects from anesthesia, other than being tired. Having said this, however,

I've also never undergone a surgery whose duration was longer than two hours. As the hands of the clock struck midnight, so did the hammer in my head, and it was relentless. I first thought it was just a wicked caffeine withdrawal, not so much. I summoned a nurse who came running in to save me. If throwing up was an Olympic sport, I'd have taken bronze—'nuf said. That was the nadir of this surgical experience, and since then, I've felt increasingly stronger with each passing day.

Thursday, I mastered the bedpan. BOOM! I also cracked one—oh my! Allow me to elaborate. I didn't trust myself to walk to the bathroom, so I reluctantly agreed with the nurse that I should go the bedpan route until I felt stronger. I cracked the very first one, *say what*?! I was mortified! The nurse apologized and said the hospital had recently switched to a different supplier and these new ones were far inferior to the previous models. After the nurse inspected it, while I was atop it, none the less, she determined the crack—no pun intended—was superficial and wouldn't impact its intended, and only, purpose. The morning-shift staff change came at seven a.m., my CCP[11]— medical aid—went from a vibrant and funny woman to a twenty-something male nursing student; they each got a chance to quarterback my bedpan—good times. I lost any regard for what the hospital staff saw of me after this experience. I simply didn't have the energy to care.

---

[11] CCP stands for certified compliance professional. To learn more, you can visit https://healthethicstrust.com/certification/ccp/ for all the specific details.

Thursday was an exhaustive blur. I went from one ninety-minute nap to another—All. Day. Long. I was getting a little delirious from lack of good uninterrupted sleep. The food was as you'd expect, lackluster. But I was able to keep it down, and I finally enjoyed some morning coffee. Around five-thirty p.m., discussions started regarding my pending release. It was ultimately up to me, and (not 100 percent sure I was doing the right thing) I made the decision to go home. My bed was calling me hard, and I couldn't deny I wanted it too. I slept well that first night at home. My body relented and sank into the myriad of pillows I had ready to make me comfortable; vivid dreams ensued.

Friday and Saturday, I was a cat. I slept. I ate. I cleaned myself with a washcloth, thank you very much. I stared at a TV for longer than I care to admit—I am now an aficionado of *Naked and Afraid*. And, on occasion, I slinked around the house to stretch my legs. All in all, it was just what this girl needed.

Then, there was Saturday night. I FREAKED OUT (insert complaint #2). There was fluid streaming from my left drain incision down my ribcage that was pink—because it contained blood—and it wouldn't stop. It got on my bed, pillows, and clothing. *WTH?!* And while (it turns out) it's not uncommon, I wasn't warned about it before I went home. I was so instantly upset upon seeing this that I burst into gushing tears. I was so shocked that I could barely take a full breath or complete a full sentence.

At 10:30 p.m., I called the hospital to speak with someone and got transferred to the resident for plastic surgery. I could tell by his voice it was the same resident in attendance for my surgery. I was so put off by his handling of the call that I hung up on him. As a side note: hanging up on someone using a cell phone is so *not* satisfying. I miss the old days when you could slam the receiver down on the base to make a point, not that I ever did that or anything, just sayin'. When I finally realized I was fine and there was no need for me to immediately return to the hospital, I did my best to compose myself and get some sleep.

Sunday was much like Friday and Saturday with two exceptions: First, there was no need for any freak out, thank goodness. Second, the sun was shining, which delivered a few degrees of warmer temps! With the beginnings of cabin fever setting in I threw caution to the wind and tucked my jammies into my furry winter boots, wrapped my neck up with a scarf, pulled on a new ear-covering hat, tucked my hands in gloves, and zipped up my parka and took a walk up and down my street, once. It felt glorious to have the sun kissing my face and fresh air in my lungs, but once was enough.

Which brings us to today, Monday, five days out of surgery. I only took one nap today, yay me! I have a nearly full range of motion in my arms, which seems freakishly odd to me given everything my upper body has been through, but, hey, I'm not going to knock it. Also, my appetite has no issues. Finally, and the strangest of all, I have no sensation across my chest.

I look forward to getting cleared to take a shower. Washcloths are acceptable and all, but nothing beats a steamy, hot shower to lather up in. I also look forward to wearing regular clothes; I love all my new matching pajama sets—all out of necessity since they're soft and button up the front—but I miss my jeans and boots.

Tomorrow, I meet with Dr. Kaufman for my first post-op visit. Fingers crossed everything is going swimmingly with my recovery; I have no doubt it is.

More updates to follow as post-op doctor visits continue and plans for my next surgical adventure are mapped out. Oh yes, I still have one more surgery to go. Still plenty of milestones left to celebrate, and celebrate I shall! Each. And. Every. One.

Until next time, high five to you!

Penny "Currently Living the Hugh Hefner Lifestyle" Casselman

We're our own worst enemy and harshest critic. Good lord, seriously? Five days out from major life-changing surgery and I was proud that I only took one nap in a day? Yeesh. I'm still taking naps, years later! Here's a permission slip from me to you: if you ever have surgery that lasts more than one hour, take a nap every single day for a month! You deserve it! And your body, no doubt, will thank you too.

Wild, Wild West

Sunday, Feb 4, 2018

For nearly two weeks, I've felt like a gunslinger. My drainage bulbs have me feeling like I've got a make-shift holster on either side. Lately, I "draw" them twice a day. They are a cumbersome, annoying, gross, but necessary part of my recovery. I've said before I don't like to hasten the arrival of a future date; however, Tuesday morning cannot get here fast enough. At ten a.m., the drains will be removed—for this go-around, anyway. Yes, I will again have these gems after my next surgery. It's my hope they'll have a far less lengthy stay than these first ones.

I'm finding it increasingly difficult to sleep. I mentioned earlier that I'm a stomach sleeper, but there is *no way* I can accommodate that sleeping position at this juncture in time. My sleeping position, combined with my need for a daily nap, doesn't help my speedy send-off to dreamland each night.

Other than my daily vexation at chasing sleep, I'm doing quite well! My appetite is good, my range of arm motion is good, and my sense of humor is still intact—lucky you!

This past week I was so happy to welcome back my dad for a week-long visit! We laughed at punny jokes and visited lots of restaurants. Lucky for me, he also enjoys sneaking in a daily nap—like father like daughter! I mentioned one day that I thought the last time we spent this much time together was when I was in high school and living at home—ah, memories. In addition to spending time with my dad, a few days later my brother also made the trek out to see me! I had three glorious days of bonding with these two together; I'm one lucky girl!

Shifting gears to medical happenings. Last week, Tuesday and Thursday, I had visits with Dr. Kaufman. Everything is looking good upstairs, and he's pleased with my progress. I was initially hopeful that my drains would be removed this past Thursday. However, their output was still above what they like to see in twenty-four hours; hence they're still hanging around, literally, until Tuesday. On Tuesday, I'll see Andrea (the APRN-CNP for Dr. Kaufman) for my drain removal. As Ricky Bobby would say, "Thank you, Baby Jesus!" I'll also receive an additional 50 cc's of saline in each expander. As Hans and Franz would say, "We want to pump"—clap—"you up!"

Once these pesky drains are gone, I plan to take a shower every hour, on the hour. They will be hot. I will use up all the hot water each time. I will be squeaky clean! It will be a fantastical day! I will also reach, stretch, and bend in every possible direction. No more tubes or bulbs getting in my way. This girl will twist and turn with complete freedom! These, too, will be glorious days!

I'm very much looking forward to a more normal routine filled with non-twenty-four-hour pajama attire, a full face of makeup, and maybe even an attempt at styling my little sprouts that sit atop my noggin!

Until my next post, a big ten-gallon tip of my hat to you!

Penny "Hi-ho, Silver! Away!" Casselman

Chasing ZZZ's Like a Champ

Monday, February 5, 2018

    Last night was a crappy night of sleep. I was up from 1:30 a.m. to 3:00 a.m. and again at 5:00 a.m. I did manage to find rest after each fitful episode, but my alarm singing at 7:30 a.m. had me hitting snooze with ease. I just wasn't feeling it this morning. I arrived at the hospital fifteen minutes past my appointment time. This tardy arrival might sound bad, but the way things run at the Cancer Care Center on a Monday, trust me when I say it's no big deal.

    First up was my meeting with Dr. Hergenroeder. Our visits are brief as there is nothing really for him to "inspect." Instead, we just chat about how I'm feeling and if I have any new concerns or questions. This visit, I did ask him, again, about the impact of my Herceptin infusions on the longevity of my heart performance. He assured me, again, that any adverse effects of Herceptin cease after the course of treatment concludes; for me, this is July. On April 10, I have an echocardiogram scheduled to gauge how my heart has been holding up after thirteen rounds of Herceptin.

Our second topic of discussion centered around my five-year stint taking Anastrozole. This is a daily pill that I can administer on my own and get filled at my local pharmacy; no need to visit a hospital for each dose, thank goodness.

Our next and most brief topic was that of me being tired and taking long naps, I wanted to make sure it was ok. He smiled and said that having just *one* of my surgical procedures would justify me still being tired. Knowing I had *two* significant modifications done to my body, he assured me that I was well within an ordinary course of recovery to nap *a lot*.

Our final and most somber topic of discussion was my need to pay attention to any aches and pains I might experience in my upper leg and head that are persistent. You see, in the event any breast cancer cells broke free and are wandering through my body looking for a new home, they have a strong preference to settle in the femur or the brain, sigh. I do realize my cancer was caught in a very early stage, and since my lumpectomy margins were clean and my lymph nodes clear, the likelihood that this will happen is very, very low. However, it's not a 0 percent chance. This concluded my topics and time with Dr. Hergenroeder.

Up next was my Herceptin infusion. My regular nurse was off today, so I had a stand-in from another location. She was sweet, and I had a semi-private room, so it all started ok. I got extremely melancholy after this new nurse accessed my port.

It hurt. It hurt because I'm still incredibly tender in the upper chest region; my port is right above my left "breast." This slight pain combined with my previous conversation with Dr. Hergenroeder about monitoring nagging pains caused me to tear up; I'm even getting a little teary eyed while typing this.

As far as I've come, I've still got a seemingly long road ahead of me. As much as I thought the cold weather would aid in my recovery, since there are no social happenings scheduled outside in the frigid temps, there is a drawback as I'm sure I do suffer, surgery or not, from a little Seasonal Affective Disorder. I know with each passing day I get stronger and that I'm a champ for making it this far. Today, however, it just all felt very heavy.

Tomorrow, two more appointments. On the bright side, I will be drain free by lunch!

Stay tuned.

Much love to you,

Penny "Time to Rock My Rose-Colored Glasses" Casselman

Having a type-A personality, I'm relentless with my need for progress and perfection, and I can be one ruthless task master. I needed to make peace with all three attributes during this adventure. I tried to give myself grace on days when I felt less than; but at times it was extremely difficult. Although I'm a firm believer in mind over matter, there were plenty of days when my physical body just couldn't rise to the occasion. And other days when my mind didn't want to focus on the positive. In both instances, I learned to sit with myself and embrace exactly what I was feeling. I knew the place I was in would pass, but I needed to experience that exact moment in order to appreciate life on the other side. Today, I'm much better at giving myself permission to slow down. As cliché as it sounds, life is certainly a marathon not a race.

Can You Hear Me Now?

Tuesday, February 6, 2018

Today, we have many reasons for celebration! First and foremost, my drains are *gone*! Woo-hoo! Yippee! High five! I cannot express how nice it is not having the bulbs just hanging around taking up space. Tomorrow, I will wear a shirt that does not have buttons and one which I will pull over my head. It is the little things!

I shaved my legs! *Yay!* Ok, yes, I could have done this a week ago, but I just didn't feel like expending the energy. Today, feeling much lighter and more agile, I sat on the edge of the tub and smoothed 'em up! I almost feel human again. You might be asking. "Penny, why didn't you just take a shower?" Great question! Truth? I could have taken a shower today, but I'm waiting until tomorrow. "Why?" you ask. For the pageantry of it all! I already spent about twenty minutes this morning taking my standard washcloth shower and hair shampoo in the sink, and I thought it would be wasteful to bathe again after just a few short hours when, in fact, I had done nothing to require a second cleaning. Well, that and I was just lazy and preferred to nap instead, and nap I did. With regards to the pageantry for tomorrow, I fully plan to enjoy a mimosa with breakfast, then shower, then maybe enjoy a celebratory mimosa after my shower, too! Cheers to me!

I received all the pathology back from the tissue extracted during my surgery—*no cancer present*! Say what? I'll say it again: NO CANCER WAS FOUND!! No cancer in my ovaries. No cancer in my fallopian tubes. No cancer in my left breast. No cancer in my right breast. I may have a celebratory cocktail tonight too, shower or not!

My Hans and Franz visit was postponed today and rescheduled for next Monday. On another inflation note, it appears I might only need two additional rounds of expansion to get me to my desired boob size, all in preparation for my next surgery. Woo-hoo! Having said this, however, there will still be a few months of full body healing required before I head back to the operating table to have my expanders replaced by my choice of silicone, teardrop-shaped, "my don't they look real" implants. Again, I'm A-ok with this.

Thank you *so much* for your continued prayers, thoughts, vibes, smiles, jokes, and words of encouragement—I cannot fathom how people make it through an adventure like this without support from friends and family.

Love to you, my friend,

Penny "I'm a Dancin' Fool Today" Casselman

The More You Know

Thursday, February 15, 2018

Have you ever contemplated how many of your daily actions can, and often do, involve your pectoral muscles? No? Then it's your lucky day! Allow me to share with you some of these everyday and seemingly benign actions.

- Opening your car door
- Closing your car door
- Shutting your car trunk
- Opening a new jar of jam
- Lifting a basket of laundry
- Closing the flip-cap on your toothpaste
- Opening a child-proof bottle of Tylenol

Ahh, the list could go on and on, but I'm guessing you get my drift; nearly everything you do with your arms can have some interaction with your pecs. Who knew? Now you do!

Indeed, I experienced a sad day last week. After putting two slices of bread down in the toaster, I realized the raspberry jam I wanted would require me to open a brand-new jar.

Grabbing it from the pantry and not thinking through my actions, I attempted to free the lid for about one second then realized this was a no-go. The jar and I had a stare down as I frantically tried to scheme a way for me to open the jar in an unconventional way that would avoid engaging my pecs; the jar won. A moment of sadness swept over me as I pondered having toast with no jam. Luckily, and thank goodness, Joe was working from home, and after a pathetic plea to have him come downstairs to assist, I was able to enjoy my piping hot crispy toast with both butter *and* jam. I've said it before, but it's the little things! My toast that day was delicious. I layered extra jam on each slice—had to show that jar who was boss.

I'm getting much better at thinking before I engage my muscles. I'm sure I'll be good at avoiding my pecs just about the same time I'm cleared to start engaging and strengthening them again, go figure.

Earlier this week, I had two doctor appointments. First up was my post-op visit with Dr. Resnick. Nothing but great news from her! My incisions are healing nicely. I've experienced no side effects from my immediate plunge into medical menopause—hip-hip-hooray on this one! No hot flashes. No mood swings. No insomnia. Nothing! In addition to all this good news, she doesn't need to see me again for a year! Say what? It's true.

My second appointment was with Andrea. Since Dr. Kaufman has more strategic matters to attend to, Andrea is the one who can administer my Hans and Franz infusion. I'm not scared of needles; I don't like to watch them being plunged in my person, but they don't scare me. Having said this, however, the syringes she entered the room with were HUGE! Think orange push-up-pop size, holy moly. I took one look at them, looked at her, and said, "That looks like a LOT of saline! I don't want big boobs!" She smiled and said it wasn't that much—50 cc's in each, to be exact—and that after this inflation, I may only need one more expansion visit to complete the presurgical prep for the final implants. To her credit, when added to each expander, the 50 cc's were hardly detectable by me and only now have me feeling a tad tighter through my pecs. Why tight through my pecs, you ask? Unlike God-given boobs that sit atop the muscle, my silicone implants will be located under my muscle. No biggie, and no pun intended, I can get through this.

I have an appointment next week with Dr. Kaufman, the man himself, to discuss my current status, selection of implants, and timing of my phase 2 surgery.

Outside of those two medical updates, here are a few additional items of note:

1. I'm still taking a daily nap. I try to squeeze one in before three p.m. since napping later in the afternoon has negative implications on my ability to sleep soundly at night.
2. I *love* my showers!
3. My hair continues to grow, just not as quickly as I would like. I'm kinda in that weird in-between fuzzy phase where it's looking slightly unkempt and not thick enough to

be fully defined and give it some style. I'm going to need some hair product soon. Wasn't sure I'd say that again, but this time it will be different than what I've used in the past and won't require a hairdryer; those days are long gone, short and sassy is here to stay!
4. I'm thoroughly enjoying shirts without buttons, jeans, and my boots! It's so good to feel like a regular member of society again.

Lastly, since yesterday was Valentine's Day, I wanted to write you a little poem.
Roses are red,
Violets are blue,
My heart is full
Because of *you*!
Kisses, gentle hugs, and a heart full of gratitude,
Penny "Maya Angelou I Am Not" Casselman

DUH!

Tuesday, February 20, 2018

Sometimes I'm a little slow on the uptake; ok, often. Call it gullible, call it naive, call it space cadet, or—as I like to refer to it—my "cuteness factor." Last weekend I had dinner with some girlfriends, and after our meal, one friend piped up and said, "This is my favorite song."

I sat quietly for a moment, listening intently, trying to see if I could identify the song. After a few moments, and realizing it was sung in a different language, I said to my friend, "How did you hear of this song?"

She laughed as she said, "I've never heard it before!" DUH, Penny!

Another time I was out to lunch with a friend who, upon walking into the Chinese restaurant said, "I have that same painting hanging in my office."

My eyes got big, and I looked at him and said something to the effect of, "WOW, that's crazy but cool. Didn't know you liked Asian art."

To which he said, "I'm kidding." DUH, Penny!

Try as I have to overcome this "cute" character flaw, alas, after forty-five years, this trait of truly believing everything people say—at least at first blush and especially from those I know well—is here to stay. In tandem with this trait is my immediate reaction to think it's is something I ate when I'm not feeling well. Two cases in point: I thought I was hung over the first time I got nauseous at a yoga flow session; nope, I get motion sick during flow yoga Every. Single. Time. The first time I got nauseous during a movie, I thought I ate bad sushi; I get motion sick when the cinematography is mostly from the vantage of a handheld camera.

And finally, another example of this "cuteness factor" from right as I was typing this entry: I just got excited to hear my phone buzz to indicate a new email. Hello, McFly—*you just sent yourself an email*! Yes indeed, is there any hope for me? I crack myself up! Moving on—and yes, there is a tie-in here.

Last week started with me feeling a little bit miserable, and by Friday, I was full-blown *miserable*! Ugh. My misery came in the form of a sour stomach and a headache. On a scale of 0–10, I started Monday with at a 2 and ended on Friday around an 8.5; honestly, I could hardly think straight come Friday as my complete focus was my stomach. All week I was struggling to identify anything that sounded appetizing. If you've never had a sour stomach, hooray for you, I'm envious, seriously! I had experienced this feeling once before while working in corporate America. My stomach got so bad my primary care physician put me on ulcer medication, oh my. I'm happy to report that five days after quitting that job, all symptoms disappeared. As you can imagine, my immediate reaction to my malady last week had me racking my brain as to what on earth had me so stressed out?! I couldn't think of anything!

Throughout the week, I had consumed half a bottle of tums, numerous Pepto chewables, DGL (which is a licorice root extract—thank goodness I found it in German chocolate flavor; *I hate the taste of licorice*), and my standard morning Nexium pill. *Nothing worked.* Finally, and thank goodness, Joe piped up and said, "Maybe it's your medication?" DUH, Penny! Why didn't I think of that?! I made a beeline for my medication summary insert, and, sure enough, I had about five of the common side effects. Whew. Of course, I identified this around six p.m. on Friday, and I was NOT about to call my doctor only to get put through to a resident; we all know how that went last time. So, I remembered my doctor's caution when he prescribed me the medication (Anastrozole), "Penny, if you get an upset stomach or a headache cut back to taking it every other day until your body gets used to it." *Why on earth* did this not occur to me last week? The only thing that changed was my taking Anastrozole—DUH!

Friday night, I skipped taking my pill and, let me tell you, Saturday was a glorious day! My nausea was down to about a 2, and my headache rang in at a cool 0! *Woot!* Then came Saturday night, and down the hatch my pill went. Sunday, started feeling bad again. Sunday night, skipped taking my pill.

Monday came, and, unfortunately, I wasn't quite feeling as spunky as I had on Saturday after I had skipped my first pill. I made sure to connect with Dr. Hergenroeder that morning to discuss my symptoms. He permitted me to go every three days for a week or so, then to every other day, eventually working up to every day. He indicated approximately one in ten women have this type of reaction; yay me, *not*. Honestly, I should be thankful. My chemo regimen had me experiencing almost zero adverse side effects, and the ones I did experience were minor. Dr. Hergenroeder strongly believes that, over time, my body will adapt to the Anastrozole, and eventually, I won't notice any side effects; that day cannot come soon enough.

Having said all this, I haven't stopped doing activities. I went to yoga on Saturday. Sunday, I met friends for brunch and that evening went out again, with a different group of friends, for dinner. Monday, I was at it again and met a girlfriend for dinner. Friends and food are essential for the soul! This brings us to today, Tuesday, February 20, in which I had two activities.

First, an appointment with Dr. Kaufman. I received another 50 cc's of saline in each expander. I asked him several questions about next steps, and here's what I can share: My next surgery, to swap out my expanders for the final implants, will take approximately 90 minutes. *Yay!* My surgery will be outpatient! *Yay, again!* Based on my desired result, today was, most likely, my last expansion. Let's keep this adventure movin' along, I say!

I have another appointment with him next week, during which we will discuss the timing of surgery and implant choices, pending I'm good with my side profile.

The second appointment: a haircut! I have a micro fauxhawk now and feel kinda awesome and badass. The top is still growing out, as intended, so the sides and back are what needed to be tightened up, and tightened up they got! I present to you the image attached.

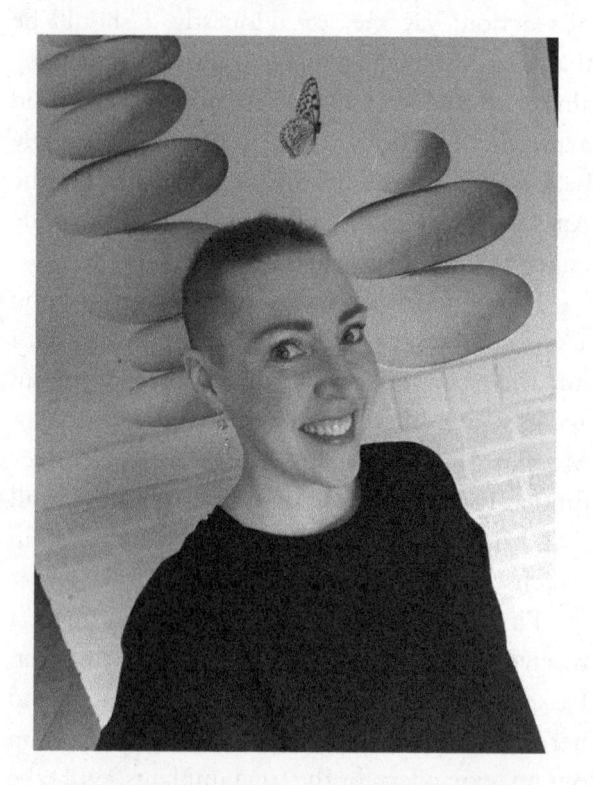

Tonight, I down another pill. "Little A," my new nickname for my Anastrozole pill, and I are going to have a talk about getting along, and it's my earnest hope, fingers crossed, we can agree to partner up for the next five years. Pretty please, Little A? Let's have some fun along the way, shall we?

Let's do this!

A big smooch from me to you!

Penny "Mr. T's Doppelganger" Casselman

Now What?

Wednesday, February 28, 2018

That's the question right now.

Now what?

With my life slowing down a bit and my final hurdles on the horizon, albeit a seemingly distant one, I find this thought bubble has nearly eclipsed my cancer focus, and I'm consumed with daily thoughts of "Now what?!"

Upon reflection, I'm not sure which thoughts are more oppressive.

There are days when I feel this adventure will never end, then I think of how far I've already come and subsequently convince myself that the end is just a blink away; *Poof*, it's July.

July, I go back to being "normal." I return to having test results that say, "Nothing to look at here, move along." I must, once again, find a sliver of normalcy and a way to fit in with other folks working to live. Now what?

It pains me to think of corporate America, the big machine that I hate and love. The last thing I want to do is explain my absence from its inner workings with the comment, "Cancer," as that's a buzzkill right off the bat! Sigh. So, I then beg the question, "What to do on my own?" Bigger sigh. I do have some ideas, no worries in that department, but developing them, having the patience to test out theories, and being persistent enough to see things through will take a commitment I have never asked of myself before. I've said it before that if I can drag my tired, sad, almost bald head out of bed for twelve weeks in a row to invite little chemical assassins to run rampant in my veins, I surely believe I can persevere for an idea birthed in my heart.

In early 2016, I was suffering from what my primary care physician assumed was an ulcer. A treatment regimen started and as weeks passed, nothing improved. One weekend I was feeling so miserable I finally made myself slow down and start listing all the reasons I could think of that were causing me distress. Was it a food, drink, or environment I was in? It seems we often can't see the reason that's right in front of us. What did I finally land on? My job. Long story short, my corporate position was raised from the depths of hell. Honestly, my experience there—combined with years spent in other corporate America settings—could fill another book with vivid illustrations to support the notion that truth is stranger than fiction. I reviewed my finances and told myself the only way I was going to get better was to quit and walk away. No amount of money was worth my health. That day, using a red pen, I circled a date on the calendar—a visual cue that would prompt me to turn in my notice. I missed my deadline by a week.

My last day of work, May 6, 2016, will be a day I'll never forget. As I was wrapping up the final transitional items, I received a text around two p.m. letting me know that my close friend, Krissy, had just died. For years, Krissy had been battling a familial

BRCA1 ovarian cancer diagnosis. I sat numb. I just had to get through this day, and then I could be sad. We all knew Krissy's time was nearing the end, but I wasn't expecting today to be the day. I powered through the last few hours of my day and drove home in silence. I had just pulled in my driveway when I received a call from my dad; he wanted to tell me he was retiring and moving to another state. My conversation with him was brief and I couldn't even mention my friend had just died or, oh by the way, I left my job today. I walked inside and went straight to bed. The next day, May 7, was my birthday, and I didn't leave my bedroom except to eat.

I had planned to take a few months off so I could plan what my next career would be; given everything I had just experienced, a few months turned into a year. In early 2017 I was laying the foundation for my entrepreneurial venture, my life coaching business. I was excited and a little stressed, but I knew if I could survive the gauntlet of corporate America, I could thrive as my own boss.

Two weeks after virtually opening my life coaching website, and almost exactly a year after Krissy's death, wham, I was starting down my own cancer path. What a biting turn of events. So again, my career needed to hit pause in support of my health and my life. I had every intention of restarting my life coaching business when I had completed my adventure. However, I knew I'd have to revisit everything I had created pre-diagnosis as my mental space had changed, and all my professional images no longer reflected the new me. And even though I had gone through so many changes, physically and mentally, I couldn't be happier with where I ended up. Life is just too short not to do, create, and experience things you love!

> Switching gears to ensure you stay up to date on my medical happenings. My final reconstruction surgery is scheduled for May 11, and yes, I'm

done with any further expansions. I previously joked about new boobs—or as I like to call them nowadays, Barbies—for my forty-sixth birthday, I've got this manifesting thing down pat! Like my surgery before, I'll have drains again and will have several follow-up appointments to ensure everything is stable and healing as expected.

Now that I'm in medically induced menopause, I've started taking calcium and vitamin D to help promote and support healthy bones. In that vein, I will be scheduling a bone density scan so I will have a baseline for comparison as my bone health is measured over my remaining lifetime.

As far as Little A is concerned, so far so good. Allowing my body to slowly acclimate to the pill's new chemistry seems to be working. Fingers crossed that as I reduce the days between pills from three to two, and then again from two to daily, my body accepts them as my new chemical state of being without throwing a fit in my stomach.

That's all for now, short and sweet, just like the sunshine yesterday.

xo

Penny "What Color is Your Parachute?" Casselman

0.804

Sunday, March 11, 2018

In decimal form, it's 0.804.

Rounding as a percent, it's 80.

In fraction form, it's 33/41.

If you were an average student, that might sound acceptable for a test score.

In my case, however, that represents the ratio of the total number of weeks since June 1, 2017, that I've either been at the hospital or in a doctor's office. Yep, thirty-three of the last forty-one weeks of my life have been scheduled with medical professionals and caregivers.

Last week was a rare week when nothing was scheduled, and it felt odd, like I forgot something. Although I had at least one activity planned per day, I still found time to stare at walls and stay in my jammies for longer than I care to admit. With plenty of idle time on my hands, my mind had a field day, and many thoughts swirled around—some cheerful, some pessimistic, and some indifferent. One of the most common comments I receive from those witnessing my adventure is this, "You are such a positive, optimistic, and entertaining writer; your attitude is simply amazing!" So, I'll let you in on a little secret, I'm not like that 100 percent of the time, sincerely. However, I have in my "toolbox of tricks" this nugget of wisdom: it takes the same amount of time and energy to dwell on the bad as it does to focus on the good. Take that to the bank!

I am gaining strength and can now swiftly open new jars of jam, or anything for that matter, with little resistance. I went to the gym this weekend for the first time since May 2017 and walked on the treadmill! It may have been just a step—my apologies for the pun—in the direction of returning to my athletic self, but it sure did feel good. I'm longing for the days when most of my walking can be done outside under a canopy of tall, shady trees. Soon enough, I know.

This week the doctor appointments begin again; however, now there are fewer weeks ahead of me than there are behind me, and that makes me smile.

A big joyful hug for you!

Penny "Keep This Adventure Moving Along" Casselman

Blarney, Blooms, and Boulders

Thursday, March 22, 2018

First, happy belated St. Patrick's Day! This gal made it out for some good ole-fashioned revelry this past Saturday, and of course, I was decked in green. It was cold, but the sun was out, friends were near, and beer was close at hand; it was a glorious afternoon. I find it entirely apropos that the Irish standard for toasting is *sláinte*, which translates as "to health"; I can certainly get behind that sentiment this year!

Next, happy spring! This one is a bit more difficult to embrace as there is still plenty of that pesky white stuff scattered all across the landscape. They say you can't appreciate joy without the contrast of sorrow, the sunshine without the dark, and so too I suppose, the budding spring without the sting of winter. This week was a Herceptin infusion, so it was back to the hospital for me. Near the end of my dose, a nurse came around with a corrugated box and handed me a small cellophane envelope, which contained three daffodil stems sporting tightly cocooned buds. She explained that a local cancer support group donated them, and they were to be shared with all cancer patients on Tuesday, my lucky day, I suppose. When I got home, I looked up the meaning behind daffodils and now happily pass this knowledge on to you. The daffodil is the first flower of spring and a symbol of hope. Today, just two days later, two of my three buds are in full bloom! Hope springs indeed!

On to boulders. Now, you may be asking yourself, "How is Penny going to work boulders into this post?" Well first, I've decided to call my girls upstairs Skippers. You see, Barbies are the grown-up and final version that I'll be receiving on May 11, and I'm considering where I'm at today to be the mucking through the puberty part of their evolution; Skipper is the junior version of big sister Barbie.

My Skippers feel like boulders, sigh. Not sure what I'm talking about? Go outside, pick up a rock, and squeeze it; yep, there you go. Mine are body temperature, but you get the idea. I'm still finding it slightly challenging to get comfortable when sleeping, but it has gotten better over the weeks. I'm doubtful I'll ever be as comfy as I once was, but I'll be healthy, and that's, after all, the end goal with this adventure. I swear the person who coined the phrase "boulder holder" for a bra must have been a woman going through breast reconstruction! Ha.

I just peeked at my calendar for the next two weeks, and, other than an eye doctor appointment, I'm free and clear of any hospital time! Hooray!

Until I write again, raise a glass!

Cheers,

Penny "Where's My Dreamhouse and Pink Corvette?" Casselman

Here We Grow Again

Tuesday, March 27, 2018

It's always been my hope that each chapter of this adventure would have a beginning and an end. I stress the word *end*.

Identification of cancer, lumpectomy, rescan, gone, *end*.

Twelve weeks of chemo ensue, hair loss begins, infusions tolerated, *end*.

Hair grows back, strength returns, eyelashes and eyebrows "peace out," eyelashes and eyebrows return . . . wait for it . . . wait for it . . . *end*? I don't think so.

Aaahhhhhh.

A few days before St. Patrick's Day, I noticed my inner eyelashes, those closest to my nose, and the corresponding eyebrows above them had departed, say what? It's true. As annoying as it was, I still had plenty of outer lashes left to coat with mascara to keep me looking like a normal person. And with my eyebrow pencil at the ready, a little filling in and no one would notice—except me, of course—that anything was out of the ordinary on my brow bone. Upon further inspection, I saw baby sprouts had already started their ascent to replace those missing, whew. I wasn't concerned.

Fast forward to Sunday, just two days ago, when I realized ALL my upper eyelashes had now decided to follow suit and join their dearly departed sisters. Seriously? I've lost all my eyelashes again?! My eyebrow brothers weren't quite as eager to leave and left about half of their rank and file around to represent; thanks, I guess. They all are being replaced much slower than I wish, but they are indeed returning. I'm back to having peach fuzz on my brows and two-millimeter long eyelashes.

I know what you're thinking, "Have you called your doctor about this?" No, I haven't. Will I? Yes. I just haven't made the time to do so. I'm not in a frantic tizzy about calling since I can confirm the lost hairs are returning. Having said this, however, I am curious what the doctor's thoughts are and would love to hear a reassuring voice tell me this isn't going to happen again and again at regular intervals. Please, oh wise doctor, oh please reassure me of this. I am crossing every appendage that this exodus of hair is isolated only to my eyes and that the ever-growing field of fuzz atop my noggin is safe.

In other news, my bone scan was the least invasive procedure I've had in the past year, and the results were excellent. I've got healthy bones for a woman of my age. Calcium on, I say!

Little A (Anastrozole) and I are now best friends forever, or for at least the next five years.

We hang out every day during dinner. Table for two, please.

I'm a little over six weeks out from my next and hopefully final surgery for this leg of the adventure. Looking this good won't last forever as another surgery will be forthcoming, but I'll have a good ten to twenty years before I have to have the girls replaced, again. Anyone care to shimmy until then?

No doctor visits this week, hooray!

The days are getting longer, and the sun is feeling warmer; yep, all signs point to spring.

Big bunny hugs and kisses to you!

Penny "Cottontail" Casselman

PART SIX

Boob Job!

My Superheroes

They're just boobs, right? Easy for me to say. I had options, lots of options. I'd say too many options. My mom, not so much.

I did a little research about breast cancer and subsequent reconstruction in the seventies so I could understand what my mom was dealing with and how it compares to my adventure. There is no comparison. That research combined with my fleeting memories and my dad sharing his memories—after being prodded by me—and what my mom endured seems nothing short of barbaric. People think I'm brave and positive and resilient—I'm quite certain my mom had me beat in spades, on all fronts. Going forward, if anyone asks who my superhero is, easy, my mom.

My secondary superhero? My dad! As if you didn't see that one coming. While losing his wife, he had to immediately take complete oversight of two little kids without skipping a beat. I cannot fathom the massive wave of overwhelm that hit him. I think I have stress and overwhelm somedays? Yeesh, I just had to pick which boob size I wanted and figure out how I was going to navigate a few months of being bald. But all my memories and thoughts on Dad, well, that's a whole other book offering a different adventure and heartwarming tales. And I digress.

There's so much I don't remember about my mom's adventure with all things cancer. But there are a few memories I hold dear. Memories of precise moments in time that leave me feeling a strong connection with my mom.

One afternoon when I was about four years old, I was playing in my room when I heard my mom call for me from her bedroom. I dropped whatever it was I playing with and made a beeline to see her. Once I crossed the threshold, I launched myself on top of her bed, which was an epic ocean compared to my little twin. It looked like an ocean, too, with the navy-blue polyester quilt that draped so neatly over the sheets and pillows. The bed was perfectly made each morning.

My mom was standing in the corner of her room in front of her small closet with her back to me. She said, "Penny, how do I look in this?" She spun around, and there she stood in a pair of shorts and a yellow and white striped tube top. I busted up, giggling, and rolled around on the bed. She turned back around to look at herself in the full-length mirror mounted on the inside of the closet door; she started laughing too. I told her she looked silly; she said she looked silly. We both had a grand ole time laughing on the bed together before she took off the tube top and put on a different, less revealing shirt. I'm sure my mom was looking for some levity, some childish innocence to help her brave and accept her new body. Laughing is, after all, good for the soul. And I have to believe she was just tired of being sad.

After my mom's mastectomy, she didn't have reconstruction. Honestly, I'm not sure if it was even an option for her. All that occupied the space where her breast had been was nothing more than a straight Frankenstein scar from the middle of her chest to just below her armpit, and the remaining skin lay tight against her rib cage. Why were we laughing? She hadn't tucked her silicone external breast mound under the tube top, so as she stood before me, her chest mimicking one squinted eye and one wide open. The tube top was a kind of pirate boob-patch, and yes, it looked ridiculous.

Well, Hello There!

Friday, April 27, 2018

My, oh my! Has it really been a month?

How are you?

What's been going on?

What's that? You wanna know about me? Well, okay then.

Where to begin? Let's start with a quick follow-up from my last entry regarding my eyelashes—wink, wink. In a nutshell, my eyelashes are doing precisely what yours do—grow, hang out a while, fall out, and start all over again. Here's the kicker, yours are old pros at this point and understand the secret to success is a staggered growth-cycle; whereas mine, they've got some training to do. You see, chemo killed my lashes in one fatal swoop, which means they're *all* following the same growth cycle at the same time. How does this translate to me? I'm likely to go eyelash-less a few more times over the next year while they find their preferred staggered rhythm. I confirmed this fact during my yearly eye exam, so a medical professional did weigh in on my perplexing question. Now, a month later, my lashes are still growing in from their St. Pat's fall out. They should hit their final stride next week, perfect timing that I'll have lush, long eyelashes to celebrate my birthday on May 7! New eyelashes *and* new boobs for my birthday? Yeesh, this gal hit the lottery!

Months ago, Dr. Hergenroeder mentioned it would take about nine months until I was back running at around 90 percent of my pre-chemo energy, and, at the time, I got a little melancholy about it. Fast-forward six months, and it's like a switch got flipped for my stamina! I can't discount the change in weather (i.e., more sunshine and less snow have drastically assisted with my rebound), but I'm buzzing around and feeling great. I still lack a majority of the strength I once had in my chest, and things like using my cordless drill and hammer can prove slightly challenging at times, but home improvement projects are, once again, progressing quite nicely.

Remember back in January when I decided nothing says "Here comes a six-hour surgery" like painting and redecorating my office, finishing the night before? Yep, just like my second and most daunting surgery back in January, I've decided that while I have the energy, and before my next major surgery, it was time to finish *every small home repair* that I've been living with for ten years. Honestly, I'm exhausted, and I have thirteen days left to complete everything. I'm also asking myself why on *earth* didn't I take care of some of these things before? *C'est la vie!*

On Tuesday, I had my pre-op touch base with Dr. Kaufman. Two sets of Barbies will be on hand during my ninety-minute surgery; it will be an on-table decision as to which set I go home with. Whoa, Nelly! Don't freak out! I won't be awake to assist in this decision, no way. Dr. Kaufman will make the determination, and I have the utmost confidence he'll select the correct pair. Trust me when I say there is only a nominal difference between the two options. It's not like the choice is between an apple and that of a watermelon; side note, I'm allergic to watermelon. HA, and true!

During my discussion with Dr. Kaufman, I asked him what the next ten years are going to look like for me and the Barbies. Here are the details:

Me: What do the next ten years look like?

Dr. K: After surgery, I'll see you the following week for a touch base and drain removal. Then I'll see you at three months, at six months, at one year, and then every two years after that.

Me: Isn't there some imaging check you'll need to perform to ensure the implants are intact?

Dr. K: Yes. Standard protocol is a checkup every two years accompanied by an MRI of your implants.

(Dr. Kaufman mentioned that most people don't do the MRI check and that after their one-year touch base, they usually disappear. I explained to him that I still wear a lower retainer Every. Single. Night. even though I finished wearing braces at age eighteen. He said I had nice teeth. I said I was a rule follower. He smiled.)

Me: So, what about mammograms? How often do I have to have them, and how do they work?

Dr. K: Umm, you don't need one ever again. There's nothing to "mamm" anymore.

(I had to chuckle at his response. Honestly, I was perplexed as to how they were going to work with the Barbies anyway. The more you know!)

Moving on. I got my hair trimmed yesterday, and I feel sassy again! Now that all follicles are firing as requested, I can start growing it out into an intentional style, not just a buzz. To reiterate, it's staying short, for sure. It's too darn easy to get ready now, and I'd much rather use my precious time to live, experience, and thrive. Sitting on a patio, soaking up the summer sun with a cocktail in my hand, chatting with friends for an extra fifteen minutes enriches my life more than standing in the bathroom blow-drying my hair!

Once again, I have doctor appointments each week until surgery, and they continue after. I've enjoyed my short stint of relative freedom from the hospital, hence my one-month absence from a journal entry; I've been busing living! My countdown again commences, and I stand at fourteen days until the next chapter in this adventure unfolds.

Thank you for your continued support, love, and well wishes.

With armfuls of gratitude,

Penny "Is That a Train or the Sunshine at the End of the Tunnel?" Casselman

Tomorrow Dawns a New Day!

Thursday, May 10, 2018

Before I dive into the litany of questions you might be wondering about tomorrow, allow me to provide a brief update about what's happened since my last post, thirteen days ago.

May 1

Once again, I made my way to the pre-surgery admissions office for an interview regarding my overall health and wellbeing so I could be cleared for my procedure, which, I can hardly believe, is tomorrow. I passed with flying colors, and the intake nurse commented, "I hope the rest of my patients scheduled today are as easy as you."

"Me too!" I said. We marveled at the beautiful weather that day and were both chomping at the bit to get outside and soak it all up. My day inside the walls of the hospital, however, was not yet over, and I immediately trotted over to the Cancer Care Center to sit for yet another Herceptin infusion. The patient load was light that day, and I got checked in, ushered back, and processed through in short order—*hooray!* I even got a private room, too, a rare treat!

May 5–7

(Sing along ensuing) You say it's your birthday? It's my birthday, too! Yeah! I had a superb weekend doing birthday things. If you can think of it, I probably did it! Oh yeah, you say? In short order: I toasted Cinco de Mayo, watched the Kentucky Derby, drank a lot, danced a little, sang like a rock star, ate cake, took in a comedy show, opened presents, opened cards, got hugs, gave hugs, talked to family, saw friends, ate out, went shopping, and got a little melancholy over the fact I've nearly hit the one-year mark of this entire adventure commencing. WOW! It was indeed a heartwarming weekend. A caveat, I found my *perfect* party skirt at Anthropologie! I can't wait to show it off when we all finally gather together to celebrate the END of this adventure!

May 8

I had a follow-up with Dr. Joseph to see how things were looking, or shall I say feeling, since my surgery. I'm pleased to report that everything is looking and feeling fantastic. Given this news, I will see Dr. Joseph again in six months and then every twelve months after that, for five years.

This brings us to today, the eve of yet another surgical procedure for this lass and, hopefully, the last.

Many of you have asked, "Are you excited/anxious/nervous/ready?" Honestly, I've struggled to describe exactly how I'm feeling about everything. On the one hand, I'm ready to keep this entire process moving along. I'm prepared to check off one more task on my medical procedure to-do list. Ready to have this all in my rearview mirror. While in the same breath, I'm not ready at all. I'm not looking forward to, once again, having a stare down with a jam jar. Not psyched up for a week of drains, sponge baths, difficulty getting comfortable, and each night chasing a few short hours of sleep. I tell myself I've done this all before under massively more dramatic circumstances and bounced back. This time around, I know what to expect. There should be no freak-outs, no calls to a resident, and no need for concern as I have planned and prepped to make my life simple for the next week.

Honestly, the considerable enigma I face is this: these Barbies will be final. There is no exchanging them for a different pair if I decide I don't like them. No refunds. Period. I told Dr. Kaufman when we met for my final pre-surgery touch base that "I don't like playing God." And I honestly meant it. We all at one time or another have wished to tweak just one thing we were born with to make us better or somehow improved. Things like a different eye color, curly hair instead of straight, a smaller nose, a longer neck, a tinier waist, broader shoulders, bigger lips, longer eyelashes, you get the idea. Speaking from experience, when faced with actually making a *real* decision at that level, it's daunting. Here's what I want to tell you: You are the *best you ever*! Don't change a thing; unless, of course, it's out of medical or psychological necessity. The Barbies will look, feel, act, and appear more natural than my current Skippers—thank goodness. I'm very much looking forward to having the final versions in place; I grow weary of being in limbo with my body image.

Finally, what is most likely top of mind for you are the details of my procedure tomorrow. I will report to the hospital at 6:45 am with my surgery planned to begin before nine a.m. I anticipate everything will occur without incident, and a glowing post-surgery report will be issued. This is an outpatient procedure (the wonders of modern medicine!), and I expect I'll be home resting comfortably well before dinner time.

Thank you for your love, support, well wishes, thoughts, and prayers.

Until my next entry, much love and gratitude to you!

xo

Penny "Are Those the Grand Tetons?" Casselman

Tomorrow Has Arrived

Friday, May 11, 2018

Good morning Team Penny! Joe here, reporting in.

Our girl is all prepped and on her way to the surgery room. As the nurse was wheeling Penny back, she was doing a royal wave to an imaginary crowd.

Yes, she is in good spirits and ready for today's procedure.

The surgery will take two hours or so. I'll keep you posted on any news I receive.

Go have a great day and know Penny's in good hands and will be home soon.

Surgery Update

Friday, May 11, 2018

Hi All, Joe coming at ya. I just spoke to Dr. Kaufman and Penny did great. She is ready to move to recovery, and I should see her soon.

I know Penny will post all the crucial details shortly, in her unique way. We appreciate all your thoughts, prayers, and support.

Here's to heading home!

Home

Friday, May 11, 2018

I'm typing this on my iPad from the comfort of my bed. Couldn't leave y'all hanging for too long on my post-surgery update.

I'm whooped. Got home at one p.m. and went straight to bed; ok, not really.

First, I changed into some comfy pajamas, took my antibiotic pill, emptied my drains, ate a piece of toast, decided my request for a single piece of buttered toast was too dry and subsequently asked for jam to be added, finished my toast, drank some water, looked at my phone, *then* went to sleep. Zzzz.

I awoke around five-thirty p.m., sat up, and requested some coffee, which, by the way, I'm enjoying right now—keeping that caffeine withdrawal headache away, thank-you-very-much. I'm still tired, and an early bedtime is in my future, but not before a "breakfast for dinner" is served and an episode of *Lost in Space* is consumed. Great show!

Thank you all for coming along for this adventure, we're rounding the corner and are now in the last stretch!

Race on, I say!

Love,

Penny "This Bed is *Just* Right!" Casselman

My first surgery sucked because of all the prep I endured. The second surgery sucked because I was immediately thrown into medically induced menopause and I went home with drains. This third surgery would be the least sucky of the three; but it still sucked because, once again, I'd be going home with drains. Reflecting back, each surgery did move me closer to a heathier life, and for that I'm thankful. The one suck-factor they all had in common? The time it would take for my body to reorient itself to a new normal and find its well of energy for more fanciful pursuits. I had done it twice before under much more challenging circumstances, and I knew at the conclusion of this surgery I'd once again stand triumphant.

Go Go Gadget

Wednesday, May 16, 2018

    Inspector Gadget, what a cool cartoon dude. He's handy, resourceful, and full of energy, just like me; well, except for that last part. Phooey.

    I have learned throughout this adventure that I underestimate the length of time my body requires to heal. Today I remind myself it's only been five days post-surgery and I should welcome afternoon naptime. My body is attempting to process what happened on Friday and adjust to my new normal; a status that cannot come fast enough. The weather is finally welcoming me outside, patios await, friends call, and my soul needs to recharge, stat.

    Yesterday I had my first post-op appointment with Dr. Kaufman. I came through the surgery with flying colors. Thankfully, there were no significant issues immediately post-op and none since. Having said this, and as noted above, I'm still finding myself tired. I mostly attribute the fatigue to my inability to find a suitable sleeping position; you see, I'm still lugging around my drains. Perhaps, just maybe, my body needs to heal too.

    Yep, I've got drains again. I was overly optimistic they would come out yesterday, but upon emptying them before my appointment, I knew it wasn't going to happen, still too much draining. It's okay; I understand why I need them and the purpose they serve. This second episode is such a blip in the grand scheme of things, I can power through a few more days. Drains are, however, some of the most annoying accessories; I prefer a sparkly necklace or a new pair of shoes!

    Speaking of accessories, I've got a new one this time around. I'm currently sporting a three-inch wide, industrial grade piece of Velcroed elastic fabric, in white. I wear it twenty-four hours a day. It sits at the top of my Barbies and runs under my armpits behind my back. Fashionably, it's not too bad; it looks like a tank top peeking out from behind any shirt's low neckline. I do, however, appear to have four boobs, say what?! The elastic band is so tight I've got every ounce of armpit fat sticking out over the top of it while the new Barbies rest motionless below. It's got to be tight, by design, as the new identical twins need to stay immobile for as long as possible so that my body builds scar tissue, like an envelope, around them to keep their directional orientation. Since the Barbies aren't round, but rather teardrop shape, orientation matters, a lot! I've been through enough; I don't need to add circus sideshow performer to my list of new skills should one, or both, decide to rotate and protrude in a manner inconsistent with gravity.

Moving on to new skills, I've now showered with drains in place. Yes, indeed, my mad MacGyver skills came in handy as I devised a way to hold the drains in place without pinning them to my fancy surgical bra. My material of choice, you ask? Decorative pink curling ribbon. I didn't choose that color for its association with breast cancer but because pink is a color I rarely wrap with, I had ample on hand in my assortment. I created a beautiful pink necklace—ok, I tied two ends of the ribbon together—on which I then pinned my drains. Confidently, I stepped under the warm and steamy water. When my shower concluded, I removed the ribbon necklace and carefully placed it on the shower handle in front of me. I then proceeded to towel off oh so gently. Why did I shower this time around with drains when I only employed sponge baths in January, you ask? I was in a melancholy state of mind Tuesday after my appointment with Dr. Kaufman. I figured if I was going to be crabby and uncomfortable, I might as well be clean, crabby, and uncomfortable. By the way, the shower felt awesome.

Surprisingly, to me anyway, I didn't lose any chest muscle strength the way I had when undergoing my boob surgery in January, hooray! I shall triumph over any jam jar, bring it! On the flip side, I did experience something new—referred pain. At least that's what Dr. Kaufman attributed my severe shoulder pain to, and I agree. This surgery was far less invasive than the first, was shorter in duration, and nothing my body hadn't previously endured. Saturday, Sunday, and most of Monday, I couldn't lift my arms more than forty-five degrees out from my body, and it was extremely uncomfortable to thread my arms through a sleeve. By the time my follow-up appointment rolled around, my arms were back to near presurgical mobility; of course, thank you Murphy's Law.

During my appointment, Dr. Kaufman said everything looked perfect. Given the vantage points I have, I must trust his vision since what I'm looking at lately is, yeah, not looking so perfect to this gal. His trusty nurse, Sharon, agreed with him, so I'll go along with their assessment, for now.

Tomorrow I call Dr. Kaufman to advise him on my drain output. I'll learn if the drains will be removed or if I get to spend more quality time with them over the weekend. I've got another appointment already on the books for Tuesday should tomorrow's output fall short for drain removal. There will be much happy dancing when these finally get the ole heave-ho!

I'm not sure how long I have to maintain the industrial rubber band around the Barbies. I didn't ask since, at the least, it would stay in place until the removal of the drains. It isn't like I don't already have two more appointments scheduled with Dr. Kaufman within the next week. I'll have ample opportunity to ask him in person at my next appointment, no rush.

In other news, I found a blouse to go with my fancy party skirt! You remember, the *perfect* one I found at Anthropologie? Spoiler alert: it sparkles like mad! Now it's just a matter of finding the perfect jewelry to accent the ensemble. I love a good accessory challenge.

That's all I've got up my sleeve for you today. More to come in the days ahead.

Cheers to rounding the home stretch, finally.
Penny "Go Go Gadget Go" Casselman

Just Hanging Around

Friday, May 18, 2018

The drains weren't ready to leave, so we'll continue to be bedfellows this weekend through Tuesday. Honestly, I don't blame them for wanting to stay a little while longer. The weather continues to improve, and this gal has patios to visit, friends to see, and cocktails to sip, so of course, they wanted to stay around for all the fun. Drains or no drains, I'm making plans and getting out.

Speaking of going out, I became acutely aware that my previous "drain apparel" wasn't going to cut it for the seventy-degree weather we had on tap last night. You see, all my first post-op items were purchased to allow me to comfortably navigate January weather in Cleveland; I wasn't about to throw on a previously purchased top only to lose five pounds sweating under its warmth on a patio. What did this mean for me yesterday? A shopping trip was in order.

Knowing these drains are only temporary, I scooped up just three new tops; that level of restraint was challenging. Ha. Each will keep me looking stylish while effortlessly hiding my sidekicks. Three tops offered plenty of pairing options to get me to Tuesday and the removal of my don't-mind-us-we're-just-along-for-the-ride drains. *Yes!*

Honestly, it's increasingly difficult for me to stay focused. I cannot stop feeling the drains at my side, thinking of them hanging around, wishing them away, and counting down the seconds until their removal. It's like I'm carrying around a cat I can't put down for twelve days, ever, for any reason. Ugh.

Tonight, I've got another patio up my sleeve; fingers crossed the weather cooperates.

A big cheers to you and the weekend ahead.

Penny "Don't Mind These Ole Things Hanging Around" Casselman

Strap In and Hold On

Wednesday, May 23, 2018

Figuratively, and literally, I've got a lot to share, so let's get to it.

Monday, I met with Dr. Hergenroeder. It had been a while since last we met, and I came prepared with a host of probing questions for him. As always, he was generous with his time and friendly, knowledgeable, and detailed with his responses.

First up was my question about blood work. You see, during chemo, numerous blood tests are ordered each week and individually reviewed before receiving any drugs. These tests and subsequent results helped to ensure my body could handle the continuing decimation of internal systems and was equipped to start recovering immediately after treatment. Once my complete course of chemo had concluded, so did my blood work, and I've always found that odd. I'm a gal who likes to review progress and see results, and I felt entirely in the dark as to where my blood counts stood months after my last chemo. I wanted to see in black and white that my body had fully recovered and successfully bounced back to its pre-chemo levels. Dr. Hergenroeder explained that since I was able to tolerate twelve consecutive weeks of chemo that my body—more specifically, blood count—was capable of bouncing back over time. He did agree it was time to check in and see where my levels were, and a blood draw ensued. Checkmark number *one!*

Next up, I needed to confirm that my calculations were correct for the timing of my *last* Herceptin infusion. Dr. Hergenroeder concurred that, *indeed*, my last Herceptin infusion would happen on Tuesday, July 24! Checkmark number *two*!

Moving on to tofu, yes, tofu. I have heard this over the years and recently from a few friends who were concerned that my vegetarian lifestyle, which includes a variety of soy-based items, may be introducing unwanted compounds into my biochemical system. Indeed, soy-based products contain phytoestrogens and selective estrogen receptor modulators—don't I sound fancy—and, if you might recall, I'm taking a drug for five years to ensure the suppression of all estrogen in my body. Fear not, dear friend, *all is safe*! It's not only safe; it's excellent for my health to continue to eat soy-based products, including tofu![12] Bring on the steamed edamame! The more you know. Checkmark number *three!*

---

[12] This very sciencey article found at https://www.ncbi.nlm.nih.gov/pmc/articles/PMC5188409/ details the benefits of soy for everyone, including you.

I never felt I had a shortage of advice; it came in the form of how to get better sleep, what I should eat, what type of bra to wear, and "I had a friend who . . . " Unless advice was coming from a doctor, medical professional, or another person who had undergone a cancer journey of their own, I tuned it out. Not in a mean way—I'd always nod in polite appreciation for another's point of view but learned to let it go in one ear and out the other. It took time, but I understood that all advice was coming from a place of concern for my well-being, and for that, I will always have gratitude.

Next, it was Dr. Hergenroeder's turn to provide insight and ask a question of his own. Recently, medical research had confirmed that when Zometa was administered to postmenopausal women after their primary breast cancer treatment had concluded, the woman's likelihood of a metastatic cancer recurrence in the bones decreased by approximately 1 percent.[13] I realize that's a lot to digest, go ahead and take a minute (insert thoughtful pause). Got it now? Without much hesitation, I said, "Sign me up!" Whoops, I forgot to let Dr. Hergenroeder ask me if I wanted to participate. Given everything I've gone through and continue to endure, there's still a possibility of recurrence. Adding Zometa to my course of proactive therapies will, therefore, reduce my chance of recurrence even further. I plan to live a long and happy life, so I'll take that additional percentage point. What's involved, you might ask? Zometa is a three-year course of infusions, given once every six months. Each dose takes

---

[13] Visit this handy page at http://chemocare.com/chemotherapy/druginfo/Zometa.aspx for additional details about Zometa.

fifteen minutes to administer; however, it does require me to visit a hospital to receive it. I'll let Dr. Hergenroeder take credit for checkmark number *four*! I soldier on.

Lastly, on Monday, I had a Herceptin infusion. Boring. Been there, done that, moving on.

This entry now brings us to Tuesday. A day which couldn't get here soon enough. I almost burst into tears, but not for the reason you might think. Sharon, Dr. Kaufman's attending nurse, and one of my favorite people to see because of her sparkling smile, upbeat attitude, firecracker personality, and genuinely caring nature, entered the room to start the appointment. We chatted, laughed a little, got caught up on all things Penny, and then she asked to see my drain discharge log. I handed her my handmade tracking chart, and her brows furrowed, oh so slightly. I knew the volume recorded most likely wasn't going to be low enough, *but* they did remove my first set of drains at nearly the same levels, so I was keeping my fingers crossed. Sharon said it was going to be a fifty-fifty chance Dr. Kaufman was going to have them stay in place for another two days; I casually replied, "Okay, if they've got to stay, they've got to stay." I forced my best half-smile. Sharon exited the room, and before the door even closed both my eyes had tears forming.

I. Cannot. Take. One. More. Day. With. Drains. PERIOD.

Seriously, I almost lost it. Not having children of my own, I can only imagine, in that immediate moment, what it feels like for a woman nine-months pregnant and two weeks overdue. I just wanted, no needed, the drains OUT! I couldn't sleep, I couldn't think straight, my back hurt, I was uncomfortable, my tops didn't fit right, taking a shower was a chore, the drains got in my way when I did anything and everything. Ahhhhhhhhhhhhh!

Three minutes later, Dr. Kaufman entered the room, looked at my drain log, for what seemed like forever, and then said, "Let's take those things out."

I let out a quiet squeal and told him, "You're my most favorite person, *ever*!"

His response? "You do recall I'm the one that put them in there in the first place, right?" I shook my head and had to smile, that Dr. Kaufman!

I felt like a new woman when I left the office. Although I did lose the drains, I still have to wear my industrial elastic Velcroed band wrapped around the Barbies. I'm just pretending I'm getting a big, strong, manly hug, all day, every day, from all of my friends and family. I have yet another follow-up appointment on Tuesday with Dr. Kaufman to see how the Barbies are settling in and if my swelling and fluid retention both begin to subside. Then, and only then, will I be able to forego the industrial rubber band.

One more update, Tuesday afternoon, I received notifications that I had messages from my doctors. I logged into the hospital's online portal to read two notes from Dr. Hergenroeder about my blood tests. Before I dive into the results, I cannot express how *tired* I've been since my surgery on May 11. I was slightly perplexed since this second surgery was far less invasive and was an outpatient procedure. I chalked up my extreme tiredness to lack of sleep from drain discomfort and my massive physical efforts to complete numerous home improvement projects before being admitted for surgery. Now, turning back to the test results, I am wickedly "under ironed" (i.e., I'm anemic). I'm surprised, like deer needing a salt lick, that my body wasn't forcing me to the nearest cast iron skillet or hand railing and making me lick it! There are times in life when you want to be an outlier, falling outside the norms for chemical balance in your body, yeah, this is not one of those times. I was promptly given a prescription for iron pills and have already taken three doses. We'll be checking my iron levels at my next visit in October.

That's all for now.

Much love,

Penny "I Got One More Journal Entry Checked off the List" Casselman

Starting in my late twenties, it took me two years and four doctors to finally nail down a faulty gallbladder. Nothing was relieving my piercing side pain, so every six months I'd find another doctor for a consult until I finally—on my fourth try—found one that, after listening to me describe what was going on said, "Have you had your gallbladder tested?" *Bingo!*

Experiencing my mom's death and navigating my own fear of dying when I got sick, I've come to be a fierce proponent for my own health. I know my body best, regardless of my lack of medical education. From that experience I embrace and believe you are the best advocate for your health. Don't quit asking the questions, because no one is going to ask them of you.

Twelve and Holding

Monday, June 11, 2018

One week after my drain removal, I had yet another follow-up appointment with Dr. Kaufman. During this visit, I was relieved to hear I could lose the super-elastic-hug-me-forever band I had been wearing since my surgery; that would be a solid nineteen days if you're counting. After Dr. Kaufman concluded our appointment, I immediately asked Sharon if I could throw the band away. She said, "Of, course!" I imagine my jubilation in pulling it off, balling it up, stepping on the trash can pedal, and tossing it out might have rivaled the delight of the women during the 1960s Bra Burning protest at the Miss America Pageant! I'm free at last; well, almost.

I grow weary of wearing a sports bra. Yes, indeed, I still have to wear a compression garment to aid my body with its creation of scar tissue around the Barbies; they can't move until their scar pocket is complete and stable. I wear one around the clock. Remember when you were told not to cross your eyes because if someone hit you on the back, your eyes would stay that way forever? I envision that if I don't wear my sports bras 24/7, that one day I'll wake up and find a Barbie decided to up, move, and relocate to my back! I jest, I jest—maybe. Honestly, they're both still retaining pockets of fluid, and if my adventure with expanders was any indication of healing time, my body will take about ninety days to absorb the excess fluid that has accumulated. I have only a general idea of how I'll look when I get to dress "normal," but so far, I'm pleased with the boob size I chose.

As I mentioned in my last post, I'm now taking iron pills to help my blood recover from whatever it is that caused my iron counts to be so low. I curtailed my prescribed dosage of one pill twice a day, down to one pill once a day. My body wasn't having any of that two-times stuff. I did a fair amount of research into plant foods that provide iron and am making sure to incorporate more of them in my diet; luckily, they're all foods I love anyway! I'll have my iron tested again in October, but I can tell you in the last twenty-four hours I've noticed my strength returning.

One tidbit I failed to mention earlier is the removal of my port. During my last appointment with Dr. Hergenroeder, I inquired how long I would continue to have my port, since my final Herceptin infusion is rapidly approaching in July. His response was "We usually remove it on the first anniversary, or thereabouts, of your last treatment." I suppose this can be viewed as a celebration, one year away, but it means I'll have this chest lump around until July 2019. My pills, infusions, and appointments are actions no one sees. My lump, however, is visible to all; just one outward reminder that my adventure continues. Honestly, it's going to get in the way of me showing off my Barbies, ha!

Since this adventure began—a little over a year ago, which is hard to fathom—I know I've collected twelve scars, and I'm hopeful my count will hold at twelve. Each one a forever reminder of what I've endured. Most of them you'll never see; unless we both happen to be basking in the sun on the same tropical island where the outfit in vogue is an itsy bitsy, teeny-weeny yellow polka dot bikini. Then, and most likely only then, will you get a glimpse of them.

Tomorrow, I'm back at the hospital for yet another Herceptin infusion. I'm excited that I can now count how many remain on one hand. Hooray for the little wins.

Until I write again, get out there and live a little—no, make it a lot!

Penny "You Think These Scars Are Bad? You Should Have Seen the Other Guy!" Casselman

PART SEVEN

What's Next?

A Good Challenge

With the most intense portions of my medical intervention behind me, it was challenging to wrap my head around what was next—normalcy. Don't get me wrong, I longed for the day my calendar was free from doctor appointments, and now that it was almost here, it felt strange. It takes twenty-one days to build a new habit, and I had just gone through twenty iterations of that; talk about an engrained pattern of habits.

I dusted off the skeleton of my life coaching website and began to apply my newfound view of life. Since embarking on this adventure I'd come to embrace these two beliefs: Everyone's journey is unique; even if we both happen to arrive at the same destination, your path looks different than mine. And life is what you make of it, so showing up every day with armfuls of gratitude, optimism, and joy is a no brainer! I know life is short and can change in an instant.

In addition to a renewed focus on my life coaching business, I also began the monumental task of moving my CaringBridge entries into the book you're now holding. I knew this wouldn't be an easy undertaking, but I like a good challenge. One of my favorite quotes is from Morgan Harper Nichols: "Tell the story of the mountain you climbed. Your words could be a page in someone else's survival guide."

I knew I was ready to start the next phase of life, and it would require a new focus with me in the driver's seat.

Countdowns Galore!

Thursday, June 14, 2018

Forty-one, forty-five, and sixty-nine days.

Forty-one days until my LAST Herceptin!

Forty-five days until we all gather to high five!

Sixty-nine days until this woman finds herself back on the beaches of Southern California!

Did you catch all that?

My countdowns have indeed begun, and I couldn't be more excited. Well, maybe when I win the lottery, I'll be more excited, maybe. Let me break it down for you.

What seems like forever ago, my Herceptin infusions started; to be exact, July 31, 2017. It was difficult for me to fathom the end of the long road ahead; mostly, I tried not to think about it. In 2017 it was one day at a time, one moment at a time, and patience—lots of patience—knowing what I had to endure. In what now seems like the blink of an eye, I've experienced a second set of eyelashes, a new head of hair, a new hairstyle, two surgeries, numerous infusions, a slew of doctor appointments, and a gazillion needle prods. I'm rounding the corner and running—not sliding—into home. In forty-one days, my heavy lifting will be done, complete, final! I'm almost in tears typing that phrase. I realize I still have a lifetime of adventure ahead of me, including five years of a pill, three years of an infusion, and yearly doctor appointments; however, they all pale in comparison to what I've already endured. It's still strange for me to wrap my head around what a medical-free calendar looks like, what it feels like to not plan trips around visits to the hospital and doctor offices. I'll adjust, don't you worry! *I got this.*

Happy almost weekend, thanks for tuning in, see you in my next post.

Cheers!

Penny "Don't Do Anything I Wouldn't Do" Casselman

This time wasn't all spent in reflection, though. I spent time planning celebrations and travels—once more to California! I was really looking forward to not worrying about doctors or appointments or tests or treatments, for sure! Envisioning what my new life would look like took some effort. I hadn't allowed myself to think much beyond the next week of activities since I had grown accustomed to believing events could change at any time. But I did find my mind wandering a bit more and getting excited about what new adventures lie ahead. I was still very much head down in getting through these last final appointments while simultaneously making strides in moving beyond all things medical.

Fireworks, Baby!

Wednesday, July 4, 2018

Just like that, it's July 4.

Yesterday, I had my second to last Herceptin infusion. Let me say that again: Second. To. Last.

You might find yourself wanting to ask, "Penny, you're almost done; aren't you so excited?!"

My response is, "Excited? More so pensive."

A year has come and gone. A year where I pushed the pause button on my life. Instead of looking toward the future, I turned my entire focus inward and wouldn't let myself plan much further than my next appointment. I recently told a friend that I've felt the past fourteen months have forced me to stand to the right on a fast-moving sidewalk, you know, those mechanical, flat moving walkways you find at the airport. I couldn't get off, was headed down a straight path and moving at speeds that felt much slower than those of the average person seemingly always passing me on the left. I'm just now starting to hear the recorded voice saying, "Caution! The moving walkway is about to end. Please take care when stepping off."

Ahhhhh! I'm about to get kicked off this ride. I'm going to have to walk for myself. I'll no longer be confined to the straight and narrow path that was laid out before me.

I can go left or go right,
or maybe not quite
in a full complete circle,
or perhaps I just might
jump up and down
all over this town.

(I feel a Dr. Seuss-ish book being born; I digress.)

I recently perused pictures of myself captured along this adventure. I was struck by how distant a memory the images were, I hardly recognized myself. All this change in just a pinch over a year. There are times it's difficult for me to wrap my head around how far I've come.

Recently, I received clearance for two things I've been looking forward to for *months*! First, I can exercise again! Like, with weights and stuff! Watch out you two-pound hand weights, I'm coming for you! Second, and more importantly, I get to wear any kind of support garments I want! Yes—that means bras. I've already gone shopping and picked up a few in store and online; I'm now anxiously awaiting their arrival! It's so refreshing to have foundation options again! On that note, I now own enough sports bras to last me the rest of my life.

Finally, and in the spirit of the July 4th holiday, I'll share this. I'm a music girl, even if I can't always tell you the artist or remember what album a song is from or when a hit was released. Music has always been a massive part of my life. Playing piano, singing next to my dad any and every evening he tickled the ivories, singing in the school choir, dancing with my girlfriends, creating routines for my dance squad in high school, to this day, I've always got something playing. When my adventure first started, I put together a playlist of upbeat music that would be my pep talk, my strength, my counselor, my it'll-be-alright, and my release when things got tough, because I knew I would need each one of those supports as my adventure unfolded.

I used to cry when I heard Katy Perry's song "Firework" in my playlist, and honestly, I teared up tonight listening to it again. I've always been in awe of lyricists and how they take human experience and turn it into a dynamic, surging, and rhyming nonetheless, body of work that you can hear with your ears but feel with your soul. At the beginning of my adventure, I knew that my fireworks would come, albeit after I endured numerous long, arduous, and demanding activities. How fitting that today, July 4, I'm nearly at my end and ready to light it up!

The countdown continues,

Penny "It's Time to Light the Fuze" Casselman

The End of an Era

Tuesday, July 31, 2018

    I was curious about exactly how long I'd been on my adventure, and as you can guess, Google came through for the win—as if there was ever a doubt it wouldn't.

    My adventure kicked off on June 1, 2017 (the day of my breast ultrasound in response to an irregular mammogram), and "ended" July 24, 2018 (the day of my last Herceptin infusion). That can be broken down in a number of different ways:

    36,201,600 seconds
    603,360 minutes
    10,056 hours
    419 days
    59 weeks and six days
    114.79 percent of a typical year (365 days)

Whoa! Quite the adventure, indeed.

    Although the 10,000 hours of mastery theory (made mainstream by Malcolm Gladwell's book *Outliers*) has, at its core, been disproven, I can't help but think, "Yeah, I'm pretty much a world class expert in the field of 'A Penny Cancer Adventure.'" Along the way, I also gleaned a few other observations and ideas during my hours of wandering the cancer landscape that may, in time, help others navigate their adventure—cancer or not.

Rewind to Monday, July 23. Being the consummate gift-giver that I am, I had been struggling with what I was going to give the reception staff and nurses who had so kindly and compassionately greeted me and cared for me at each step along the way. They made my appointments there not only bearable but, at times, quite enjoyable, as far as anything is enjoyed during a cancer diagnosis and subsequent treatment. In true Penny fashion, an idea came to me the day before my last Herceptin infusion was to commence: a painting! "Time to go shopping!" I exclaimed. You see, I had no small canvases on hand and decided I also needed additional brushes to create my mini masterpieces.

I found everything I needed at my local Michael's Craft Store, thank goodness for one-stop shopping, and even discovered some things I didn't know I needed to complete my gift presentation! Newly purchased items included cute gift bags, an assortment of sixteen acrylic paint colors, mini easel stands so my recipients could display their personalized art, and some additional canvases for future painting projects.

Next begged the question of what to paint? In general, I'm not a big fan of pink, especially the pink associated with the ribbon color for breast cancer. I'm not an exacting artist. Ask me to draw a picture of what you look like, and you may find yourself sorry you asked. My art appreciation leanings have always been to the abstract. Artists like Kandinsky, Miró, and later works by Picasso are some of my favorites.

Although pink isn't necessarily "my thing," I thought it best to represent the ribbon in my painting since it does, without question, universally identify the type of cancer my adventure was all about. I present to you the finished pieces in the following image. A caveat, I wasn't "moved" to paint until eleven p.m., and in true Penny fashion, of course, finished around one a.m., *oh my*!

Tuesday, July 24, finally arrived. Thank goodness I had planned to arrive at the hospital around two p.m., as my night of painting masterpieces left me one sleepy girl this morning. I enjoyed lying in bed until around ten a.m.; I had to squeeze in as much beauty sleep as I could muster for my last Herceptin since a girl's gotta sparkle for an event as big and momentous as this! I selected a sparkly and chunky hematite necklace and a wicked-cool pair of Guess stilettos I had purchased years ago for a New Year's Eve party. Neither item had seen the light of day for years, and they were both as excited as I was to make an appearance on this significant day! Not to mention, I knew the medical staff would expect nothing less from their cancer fashionista on her last infusion. As expected, my shoes were a hit, and so were my gift bags and paintings!

Penny Casselman

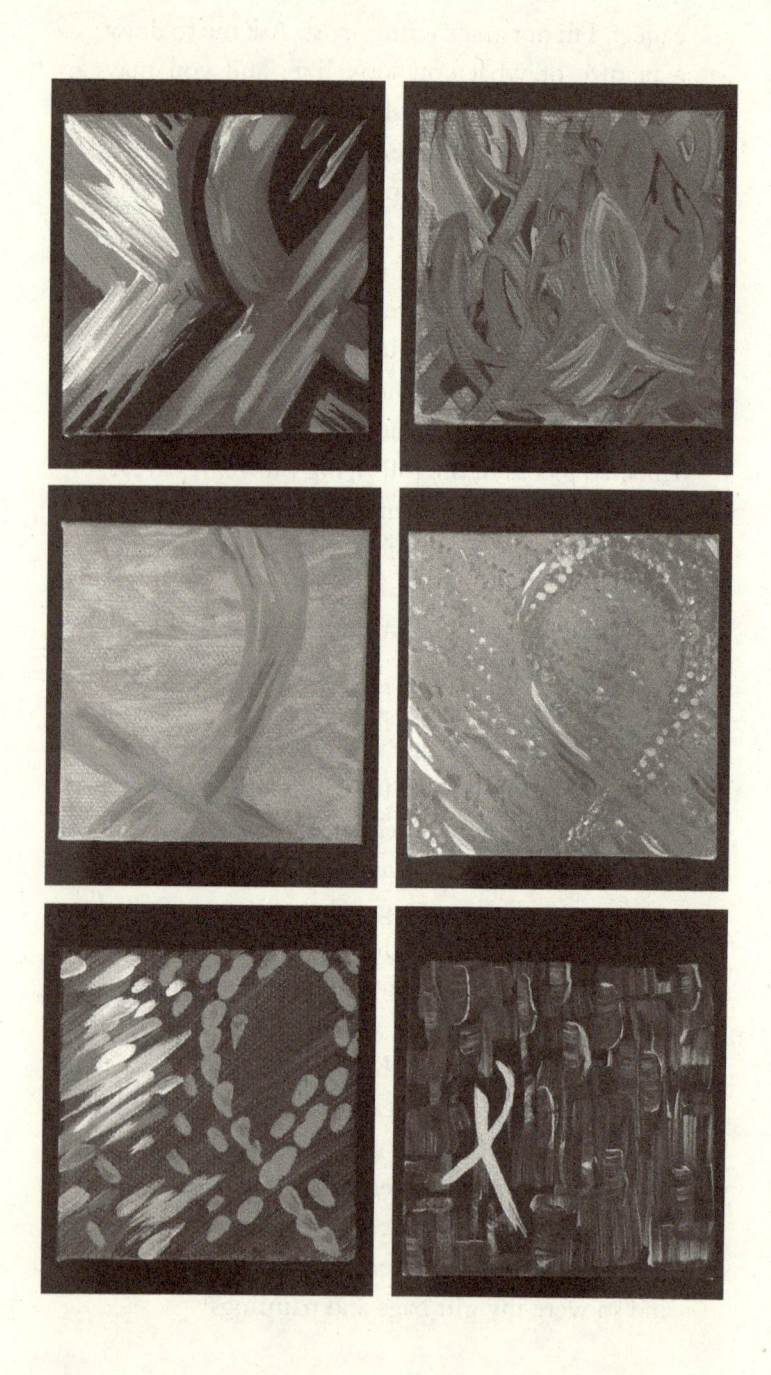

When my Herceptin infusion had concluded, and after the drip had been "unplugged" from my port, I got to ring the brass bell, signifying a person's last cancer treatment, served up on a silver platter no less, *ooh la la*! There was hardly a patient left at this time of day, three-thirty p.m., but the ringing was all for me anyway, so ring loud and long I did. The nurses and staff that accompanied me on each leg of this adventure surrounded me in an ocean of smiles, claps, and cheers. It was surreal.

I gathered up my things and started to make my way down the hallway and toward the exit, a path I had walked so many times before. A few steps into my walk, I stopped and did a 180 to issue an address to the nurses and staff. I don't recall, exactly, what I said, although I know I used words like grateful, thankful, happy, and phrases like "your work is important" and "you are the reason I made it this far." I teared up. They teared up. Before I would let the tears stream down, I pulled it together and beamed a grateful smile for everyone there. Heck, I still had a winery to visit—a little celebratory cheers was in order to mark this momentous milestone! What little makeup I had slapped on that morning was not about to run down my face before I had to make another appearance in a public venue.

As I opened the door to exit the treatment area, Tierra was holding her cellphone high, blasting Kool & The Gang's "Celebration." I gave her a big bear hug and proceeded to dance my way to the elevator! My heart was full.

Post-treatment celebration continued at Sapphire Creek Winery. I timed it perfectly; the winery opened at four p.m. and we arrived at 4:10 p.m. A few savory appetizers, several glasses of pinot noir, and a chilled glass of red sangria helped to round out my celebration; we headed home around six-thirty p.m. Our neighbors were outside when we pulled in the garage, and since I was feeling pretty good, I invited them over. My celebration continued on our patio until the sun went down. All in all, I couldn't have asked for a more perfect end to my cancer adventure.

Next up was Saturday, July 28—the "Celebrate Penny's Adventure" party!

Speechless.

Touched beyond words.

Cheeks sore from smiling and laughing all night.

Friends from all eras and areas of my life represented.

Family in from out of town.

New sparkling party outfit in full effect.

Hugs upon hugs all around.

My heart overflowing with gratitude.

Humbled.

The end, not really.

Ooh, you might be asking yourself, "What's this woman up to next?" Well first, I've got another trip scheduled to visit my aunt and uncle in Southern California, departing August 21. In between celebratory outings with them, I'll also be chillin' like a villain, taking afternoon naps, putting my toes in the sand, basking in the sunshine, finding myself mesmerized by sunsets over the ocean, breathing in the salty air, and lots and lots of nothing—in addition to finishing my coaching website and making plans for world domination so, really, not a lot.

And writing. My future will be filled with lots and lots of writing! In preparation for my book, I took the time to copy all my journal entries into a Word file; the resulting document is seventy-five pages long. Those are 8.5"x11" pages with 1" margins. Holy cow, Batman, that there's a book before I even pen another supporting word.

Although this adventure has now concluded, another is just around the corner, and I couldn't be more excited about what my future holds. I do know this, vistas, experiences, food, drink, gratitude, love, growth, and relationships will be the focal point of each decision I make. And if hindsight has taught me anything, this new adventure will far surpass my wildest dreams; I only need to trust the unfolding of events before me and listen intently to what the universe whispers.

With love beyond measure for you,
Penny "Stay Tuned" Casselman

It's Official

Tuesday, August 7, 2018

I succumb every morning to bed head! My hair has finally grown out to a length that a night spent tossing and turning on a pillow has an impact. Right before I brush my teeth in the morning, I attempt to make my sprouts as crazy as I can. Envision a Mr. T mohawk, the front man Mike Score of A Flock of Seagulls, or the ever-vibrant Troll Doll updo. It's a great way to start my day; a little levity goes a long way to promote an optimal and positive outlook on life.

You might be thinking, "You're not just sharing with us you have bed head, right? So, what do we owe this pleasure of an update so soon after your party to celebrate the end?"

My posts will indeed slow down given the duration between doctor visits and lack of significant changes to my appearance, energy, and overall health status; however, given a recent discovery, I find myself wanting to share.

A few weeks ago, in addition to waking up with epic cases of bed head, I also started waking up with stiff hands. The first time this happened, I thought, "What the heck sleeping position was I in last night to cause this much discomfort?" Although my hands loosened up as the day went on, the stiff sensation was never gone. Every subsequent day, I'd wake up with the same feeling, and on occasion, the discomfort also presented itself at the top of my knees, ugh. I started to analyze everything I had ingested over the preceding days. Had I used too much salt to flavor my food? Had I selected some items that contained too much processed sugar? Had I drank too much alcohol? Since the dog days of summer are upon us, I thought the combination of one of those factors with heat and humidity might have caused some swelling in my hands, even though there was no visual evidence of any swelling. Then, one morning I woke to find my hands feeling as if I had gone twelve rounds in a boxing ring with a brick wall, oh my! Something just wasn't right, and it was off to the Google machine to find some answers. Sure enough, this condition called arthralgia is linked to my medically induced menopause coupled with my five-year prescription of Anastrozole, sigh. After scanning an article from the National Center for Biotechnology Information (NCBI) site, I had a lot to digest—emotionally, physically, and scientifically.[14]

---

[14] If you're interested in reading the article, it was written by C. Thorne and titled "Management of Arthralgias Associated with Aromatase Inhibitor Therapy." (DOI: https://doi-org.proxy.uchicago.edu/10.3747/co.2007.152)

Before I continue too far down this rabbit hole, I can share with you that I've already made an appointment to meet with Dr. Hergenroeder to discuss approaches to lessen my joint discomfort. You see, although I love Google for all the knowledge it imparts, digging too far can, at times, cause concern where there should be none. The single article from NCBI confirming this is a known side effect of my therapies was enough for me; thank goodness I hadn't sleepwalked and wandered off into a boxing ring! Armed with just enough knowledge, I'm choosing to dive more in-depth with my doctor.

Back to my arthralgia discussion. To say I was okay with this discovery would be a lie. I was bummed. Super bummed. Eyes welled up bummed. On the verge of crying, bummed. Seriously? Some other malady I have to deal with? What doesn't kill us makes us stronger, right? *Right?*

Honestly, I had never heard or read the word arthralgia before, so, yes, I did a little more research to bring clarity to what this strange new word meant. In a nutshell, arthralgia is to arthritis just as a square is to a rectangle, meaning if you have arthritis, you also have arthralgia but not necessarily the other way around.[15]

The article I read said the side effects of taking Anastrozole are the primary reason women stop taking the drug. I'm not there yet. It would take

---

[15] You can visit http://mathcentral.uregina.ca/QQ/database/QQ.09.07/h/odette1.html to understand the mathematical reference and visit https://www.healthline.com/health/rheumatoidarthritis/arthralgia to understand the comparison of arthralgia to arthritis. You're welcome.

a lot to get me to stop taking this drug as the preventative work it does to dissuade any future cancer reoccurrence far outweighs the stiffness I feel. Not to mention, I may have natural actions I can take to lessen or resolve the joint discomfort I'm experiencing, hence my appointment to discuss this with Dr. Hergenroeder.

This adventure is undoubtedly a marathon and not a sprint. Have I mentioned that I'm not a fan of running in general?

Fourteen days. Just fourteen days until I find myself on the shores of the Pacific Ocean, watching the tides come and go, the sunrise (rare for me), the sunset (easily accommodating), and feeling the warmth of the sun and the grit of the sand between my toes. Pure bliss. Perhaps somewhere in there, I'll also find my cure for stiff hands and knees.

With grace and perseverance,

Penny "This Troll Doll is Beach Ready" Casselman

Since being diagnosed with cancer, my outlook on facing health issues hasn't really changed. Going forward, I'd still embrace these three ideas: First, you know your body best. Period. Second, find medical staff you trust and let them do their job. And third, show up and do the work prescribed. And by "work" I mean take the meds, have the surgery, and do the therapy.

I know there will always be days that feel heavy, unknown, and uncertain, and it's ok to feel overwhelmed. But with the right support in place, you can navigate uncharted territory.

The Letter S

Tuesday, August 28, 2018
    Sunshine
    Seventies
    Sunnies
    Sunscreen
    String bikini
    Sandals
    Sips
    Sand
    Surf

These and so many more are in my future until September 24; look at that, another *S*!

Taking a step back to the week before my departure, here are a few medical updates to digest.

First, a Dr. Kaufman plastic surgery update. The Barbies are doing great, according to him. I'm still adjusting to how they look, how they move, and how they feel. I'm finding it difficult to remember what my original boobs were like, which, I suppose, is a good thing. To compare my biological boobs to what I have now or long to have them back is wasted effort. For goodness sake, the original models tried to kill me. I'll keep the Barbies, thank you very much, for all their perfect imperfections.

And a Dr. Hergenroeder oncology update. Remember my stiff hands and knees? Well, I was given the okay to suspend my Anastrozole for the month I'm in California. He's quite confident that my symptoms will completely subside within approximately two weeks. I can share that although they are still a little stiff, they do seem to be headed in the right direction, and I have every confidence that I'll have a full joint recovery. Side note, only about 25 percent of women have this reaction to Anastrozole, of course. Two other medications can substitute for Anastrozole, and I'm sure I'll be signing up for one of those immediately upon my return.

I had an amazing month visiting my aunt and uncle. A welcomed change of scenery, climate, and activities was a great way to reset my frame of mind and get me thinking about my future. And while most of it, thankfully, was a blissful vacation free of cancer related thoughts, there is one event that warmed my heart, and brought symbolic closure to my adventure.

On Saturday, August 25, just four days after arriving in Southern California, my aunt, uncle, and I walked to a local Italian restaurant. There we feasted on a *ton* of Italian food! This night was our first night eating out and was deemed the default "party" to celebrate my "End of Penny's Cancer Adventure." We were tucked away in a cozy corner, bathed in light as if it came from the moon, and serenaded by some Italian music piped in through the overhead speakers. Above our heads were hundreds of Chianti bottles suspended from the ceiling, each with a unique message penned on the bottle's straw covering. We asked our waiter about their significance, and he said if we purchased a bottle of their Chianti, we, too, could compose a message and have our bottle suspended. Of course I said, "We'll take a bottle, thank you!" We had no trouble polishing off the wine—as if there was even a worry we wouldn't finish the bottle on such an occasion. At the conclusion of our meal, our server dropped off the bill and three Sharpie pens with which we could create our masterpiece.

 I observed my aunt begin to pen our message on the bottle, and I immediately began to recall all the appointments, infusions, and surgeries I've gone through that proceeded this celebratory night. All those memories coupled with several glasses of wine, and I started to cry. Our server returned to ask where we wanted the bottle hung, and when he saw the bottle's message and saw me crying, he looked at my aunt and said, "Penny?" as if she was the one who had overcome the diagnosis.

 My aunt quickly corrected him and said, "No, my niece," and she hugged me.

 Our server's expression promptly shifted from jovial to a very caring and warm smile, and with extreme sincerity he offered his congratulations and admiration for my journey. He then said, "I'll hang the bottle right over your seat, like a happy halo for you in celebration of your journey." Best. Server. Ever. My heart was full that night.

Just like that, you've reached the end of this journal entry.

Wishing you a sunny, savvy, and spectacular rest of the week!

Penny "SPenny" Casselman

This is Life

Thursday, September 27, 2018
    Flip-flops have turned into socks.
    A bikini is now a sweatshirt.
    Sunshine has turned to clouds and rain.
    Grains of sand are now stacks of mail.
    What a difference three days make.
    It was bittersweet to return home on Monday. I looked forward to all the familiar things I knew, my car, my office, my city, but I was certainly going to miss all my newfound friends, activities, and weekly routines I had established while in California. My skin reflects a slight kiss of sun, and if you look hard enough, you can see a faint watchband outline to support the fact that I was visiting a sunnier climate. My legs aren't gleaming white like they were pre-trip, and I may just have a few more freckles on my cheeks. Yep, Southern California vibes are palpable.

My trip to California was relaxing and refreshing, but now that I was back in Cleveland, it was time to start thinking about the future. I had some plans—this book is the product of one of them!—but I gave myself room to figure it all out.

I'm embracing progress over perfection, a concept I've spent a lifetime trying to comprehend but was never fully able to embrace—until now. *Nothing is perfect*. Not life, my health, my relationships, my taste in wine, nothing. So why should I expect my business, my impact on the world, my ability to help others to be perfect before I even start? That's just silliness, I say! I'll have bumps along the way, missteps to compensate for, and lots of learning to do, for sure. Be patient with me, and I'll do the same with myself.

What is life if not the experiences we gather, the adjustments we make, the love we spread, and the lives we impact along the way?

I'm so looking forward to my next adventure and hope you, too, will join me.

With so much love and gratitude for you that I'm bursting at the seams.

Penny "Namaste" Casselman

Flashback

Wednesday, July 17, 2019

Did you just have a flashback too? Feels like old times, no?

I'm sitting at my computer, quiet. Lights low, sun going down, and reflection on my mind.

Where are my manners?! Hi there! Have you had a good week thus far? I hope so. It's summer—dang it—and you should be soaking it all up. Cherish these times, you'll need to call on them when sub-zero temps hit. Until then, we dance in the sun!

I'm a little rusty at these journal updates—after all, it's been ten months since the last—so thanks, in advance, for your patience.

Before I go any further, this is not an update filled with bad news—quite the contrary! What's got me so pensive? A number of things. So let's dive in.

I'm actually getting a little teary-eyed typing this. Composing a journal entry in CaringBridge at night when I'm really quite tired—well, kinda makes me feel like I'm back at the beginning of all of this. Having conversations in my head about what I want to share while staring intently at my screen and bathed in the blue light of my monitor—promising myself I'm not going to bed until this is done. Memories.

Last Friday I was supposed to have my second (of six) Zometa infusions at the hospital. I had purposely not scheduled anything on my calendar Friday, Saturday, and Sunday since the first Zometa infusion had me feeling under the weather for two days after infusion. Well—who knew that a hospital pharmacy could run out of Zometa?! Yep, they did. *Ugh!* Seriously? The pharmacist placed an order and said I could come back Monday to pick it up. Yay. NOT. So, it cost me three dollars in parking fees to be told I'd have to come back Monday and do it all over again.

This meant I had to find activities to do in short order if I was to consider my weekend a success. A gal with my appetite for social gatherings took on the challenge—and nailed it! I enjoyed some patios, cocktails, friends, and sunshine. You?

Monday arrived and I was off to the hospital—again. Everything went according to plan this visit, thank goodness. There could be no further delays—not one! I had everything planned out. Made decisions. Booked appointments. This was happening—Monday!

Why the urgency? The demand that Monday be the day? Because two months ago, after some deliberation and tears, I scheduled an appointment with Dr. Kaufman to have my port removed on Tuesday, July 16.

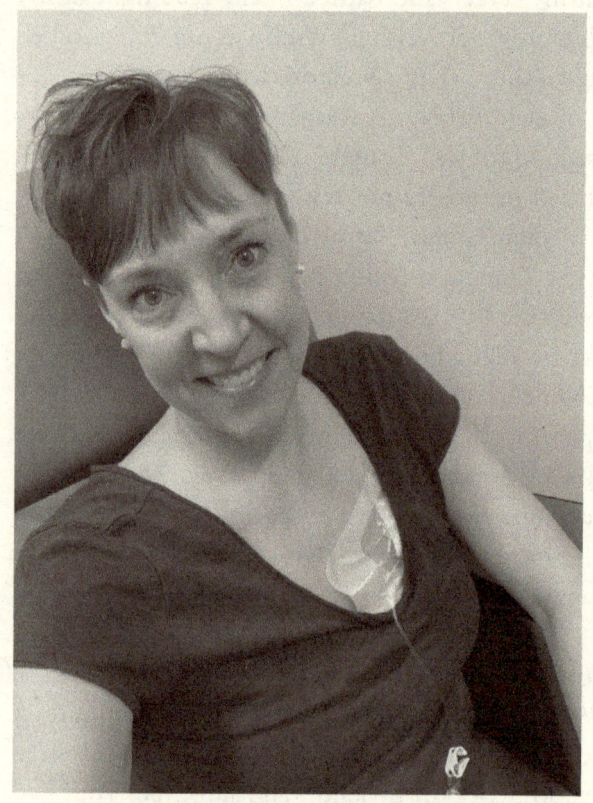

This picture is me during my LAST port use ever, on that Monday!

Today—I feel a few ounces lighter. But I also feel like someone sucker-punched me in my upper left chest. When driving my car, I've had to hold the seatbelt out a tad since, of course, it crosses exactly where my stitches are. I'm sure later this week it will turn into a nice shiner! And over the course of the next year—fingers crossed—I'll hardly even notice I had an implant there at all.

No pale-blue-purple bump protruding from my chest. No tiny little bump across my collar bone. Just the anatomy of a normal run-of-the-mill woman. Ok—except for the parts of my anatomy that have been evicted, of course.

Did you pick up on the above reference to tears? Not a quiz. Promise.

While I pondered the timing of my port removal, I cried a lot—red eyes like tomatoes and mascara running down my cheeks kinda cry. Holy crap! I hadn't realized how attached I got to it. But, just like the cancer mass before it, the time had come for my port to be evicted. My port was a part of me for two solid years. Two. Years. It never took a day off, wasn't sad or hurt or lonely; it didn't complain once. It's a little piece of tech that helped get me through all my infusions including chemo, Herceptin, and two of Zometa. I knew the drill involved to have it accessed by a nurse and what it felt like. Now my remaining Zometa infusions (my next one is in January 2020) will be administered the old-fashioned way, via a vein in my arm. See, you and I aren't so different after all. Change and the courage to accept it, gracefully—lesson learned.

With a sweet bearhug for you!

xoxo

Penny "Winnie the Pooh" Casselman

Conclusion

I used to think everything I'd gone through would have made me an unstoppable force of nature. That I'd look at life with reckless abandon, embrace courage I had never known, and rise to levels I couldn't have imagined. But as time presses on, I catch myself entertaining some of the same annoying thought patterns I had before this adventure began. Self-doubt, uncertainty, and malaise still follow in my shadow and attempt to derail my efforts from time to time. But, luckily, their visits are brief. You see, they know I don't have the same tolerance for such uninspired company. The revelation with this admission? It means I'm still human, despite all my surgeries.

A frequent question throughout my adventure was this, "Penny, do you have new perspectives on life?" After many moments spent in reflection, I can endorse these three principles: always sparkle, embrace gratitude, and radiate optimism. Let me break them down for you.

Always sparkle. For me, whether it was with high heels, statement necklaces, kind words, or just a smile, a little sparkle went a long way to brighten my days—even those that were heavy with tasks and oppressive in thought. I've seen, firsthand, that when you sparkle, the world sparkles with you.

Embrace gratitude. There were a gazillion things—alright, maybe more like tens of things—that I could have complained about, focused on, or thrown hate toward. But, deep down, I knew life is what you make of it—so showing up every day with armfuls of gratitude and joy was an easy decision! I found gratitude for life, for fake boobs, for medical advances, and for the friends, family, acquaintances, and strangers that crossed my path. Gratitude helped me realize that the life I'm living, regardless of circumstance, is already quite remarkable.

Radiate optimism. I realized quickly that when an unexpected event radically alters your life, it's easy to hold onto fear, want to retreat, and feel hopeless. But living a life devoid of excitement for a future, well, my friend, it's not how this gal is choosing to live. I've still got a lifetime of monitoring my health, but I'm fiercely optimistic that what's waiting for me will far surpass my wildest dreams. And when challenges cross my path in the future, I'll just go on another adventure.

Do I still think of cancer and the possibility of recurrence? You bet—nearly every day. On the rare occasion that I do shake free from the thought of cancer, I'm often quickly snapped back to it by some external force. A television ad will promote a new drug providing life-extending treatment for women with cancer. A TV show or movie will suddenly introduce a cancer narrative for a character. Or I catch a glimpse on social media of someone discovering they, or a close acquaintance, just received a cancer diagnosis; their adventure about to begin. Even driving around, I'll see license plates and bumper stickers sporting a pink ribbon. And let's not forget, the entire month of October is devoted to breast cancer awareness.

Throughout 2019 I was head down in writing this book, updating my website, and finding my stride. I was excited to make 2020 my comeback. Then, COVID-19. Trust me when I say it felt like a cruel joke. I had just spent years evicting cancer and taking every precaution to prevent its recurrence, looking forward to getting back out there, socializing with friends, and building my business. Then, BAM—I'm staring down 2020 with a similar trepidation for my future. This time it's not an internal foe I'm facing, but a silent, invisible, and deadly one roaming out in the open—a bizarre and harsh twist of events.

But here's the thing—there's not much in life that you can count on with 100 percent certainty. I can only think of three. One is taxes; the second, death. And the third? Change. The better I've gotten at embracing change, the more happiness I've experienced, and the more excited I am about my future.

Now it's your turn! Get out there and embrace life—you got this!

Chronology of Events

7   CELEBRATE: My 45th Birthday!

25 PROCEDURE: Mammogram

26 EVENT: Received Request for Breast Ultrasound

MAY 2017

SUN	MON	TUE	WED	THU	FRI	SAT
	1	2	3	4	5	6
7	8	9	10	11	12	13
14	15	16	17	18	19	20
21	22	23	24	25	26	27
28	29	30	31			

JUNE 2017

SUN	MON	TUE	WED	THU	FRI	SAT
				1	2	3
4	5	6	7	8	9	10
11	12	13	14	15	16	17
18	19	20	21	22	23	24
25	26	27	28	29	30	

1 PROCEDURE: Breast Ultrasound

6 VISIT: First Appointment with Dr. Hauer

7 PROCEDURE: Biopsy of Mass in Breast

13 VISIT: Appointment with Dr. Hauer

15 VISIT: First Appointment with Genetic Counselor (Elizabeth)

20 VISIT: Pre Surgical Evaluation

23 SURGERY: Lumpectomy & Sentinel Lymph Node Removal

30 VISIT: Post-Op Appointment with Dr. Hauer

30 VISIT: Appointment with Genetic Counselor (Elizabeth)

JULY 2017

SUN	MON	TUE	WED	THU	FRI	SAT
						1
2	3	4	5	6	7	8
9	10	11	12	13	14	15
16	17	18	19	20	21	22
23	24	25	26	27	28	29
30	31					

- 3   VISIT: First Appointment with Dr. Resnick
- 6   VISIT: First Appointment with Dr. Joseph
- 13   VISIT: First Appointment with Dr. Hergenroeder
- 18   VISIT: First Appointment with Dr. Kaufman
- 19   PROCEDURE: Breast MRI
- 21   VISIT: Cognitive Research Study
- 24   PROCEDURE: ECHOCardiogram
- 25   PROCEDURE: Chest Port Placement
- 29   VISIT: Wig Salon Appointment
- 30   ACTIVITY: Buzz Cut!
- 31   INFUSION: First Chemo
- 31   INFUSION: First Herceptin

AUGUST 2017

SUN	MON	TUE	WED	THU	FRI	SAT
		1	2	3	4	5
6	7	8	9	10	11	12
13	14	15	16	17	18	19
20	21	22	23	24	25	26
27	28	29	30	31		

- 7   INFUSION: Second Chemo
- 7   VISIT: Appointment with Dr. Hergenroeder
- 14   INFUSION: Third Chemo
- 21   INFUSION: Fourth Chemo
- 21   INFUSION: Second Herceptin
- 28   INFUSION: Fifth Chemo
- 28   VISIT: Appointment with Dr. Hergenroeder

5	INFUSION: Sixth Chemo
11	INFUSION: Seventh Chemo
11	INFUSION: Third Herceptin
14	VISIT: Appointment with Dermatologist
18	INFUSION: Eighth Chemo
25	INFUSION: Ninth Chemo
25	VISIT: Appointment with Dr. Hergenroeder

SEPTEMBER 2017

SUN	MON	TUE	WED	THU	FRI	SAT
					1	2
3	4	**5**	6	7	8	9
10	**11**	12	13	**14**	15	16
17	**18**	19	20	21	22	23
24	**25**	26	27	28	29	30

2	INFUSION: Tenth Chemo
2	INFUSION: Fourth Herceptin
9	INFUSION: Eleventh Chemo
16	INFUSION: Twelfth Chemo
16	VISIT: Appointment with Dr. Hergenroeder
24	INFUSION: Fifth Herceptin

OCTOBER 2017

SUN	MON	TUE	WED	THU	FRI	SAT
1	**2**	3	4	5	6	7
8	**9**	10	11	12	13	14
15	**16**	17	18	19	20	21
22	23	**24**	25	26	27	28
29	30	31				

9	VISIT: Appointment with Dr. Joseph
13	INFUSION: Sixth Herceptin

NOVEMBER 2017

SUN	MON	TUE	WED	THU	FRI	SAT
			1	2	3	4	5	6	7
8	**9**	10	11	12	**13**	14
15	16	17	18	19	20	21
22	23	24	25	26	27	28
29	30	31				

DECEMBER 2017

4 INFUSION: Seventh Herceptin
4 VISIT: Appointment with Dr. Hergenroeder
4 VISIT: Appointment with Dr. Resnick
5 VISIT: Appointment with Dr. Kaufman
26 INFUSION: Eighth Herceptin

SUN	MON	TUE	WED	THU	FRI	SAT
					1	2
3	4	5	6	7	8	9
10	11	12	13	14	15	16
17	18	19	20	21	22	23
24	25	26	27	28	29	30
31						

JANUARY 2018

16 INFUSION: Ninth Herceptin
17 VISIT: Pre Surgical Evaluation
24 SURGERY:
   Bilateral Mastectomy, Placement of Expanders, & Salpingectomy-Oophorectomy
30 VISIT: Post-Op Appointment with Dr. Kaufman

SUN	MON	TUE	WED	THU	FRI	SAT
	1	2	3	4	5	6
7	8	9	10	11	12	13
14	15	16	17	18	19	20
21	22	23	24	25	26	27
28	29	30	31			

FEBRUARY 2018

SUN	MON	TUE	WED	THU	FRI	SAT
				1	2	3
4	**5**	**6**	7	8	9	10
11	**12**	13	14	15	16	17
18	19	**20**	21	22	23	24
25	26	**27**	28			

- **1** PROCEDURE: Chest Drains Removed
- **5** INFUSION: Tenth Herceptin
- **5** VISIT: Appointment with Dr. Hergenroeder
- **6** PROCEDURE: Adding Saline to Expanders
- **6** VISIT: Post-Op Appointment with Dr. Joseph
- **12** PROCEDURE: Adding Saline to Expanders
- **12** VISIT: Post-Op Appointment with Dr. Resnick
- **20** VISIT: Appointment with Dr. Kaufman
- **27** INFUSION: Eleventh Herceptin
- **27** VISIT: Appointment with Dr. Kaufman

MARCH 2018

SUN	MON	TUE	WED	THU	FRI	SAT
				1	2	3
4	5	6	7	8	9	10
11	12	13	14	**15**	16	17
18	19	**20**	21	22	23	24
25	26	27	28	29	30	31

- **15** PROCEDURE: Bone Density Scan
- **20** INFUSION: Twelfth Herceptin

APRIL 2018

SUN	MON	TUE	WED	THU	FRI	SAT
1	2	3	4	**5**	6	7
8	9	**10**	11	12	13	14
15	16	17	18	19	20	21
22	23	**24**	25	26	27	28
29	30					

- 5   VISIT: Eye Dr. Appointment
- 10   INFUSION: Thirteenth Herceptin
- 10   PROCEDURE: ECHOCardiogram
- 10   PROCEDURE: Adding Saline to Expanders
- 24   VISIT: Appointment with Dr. Kaufman

MAY 2018

SUN	MON	TUE	WED	THU	FRI	SAT
		1	2	3	4	5
6	**7**	**8**	9	10	**11**	12
13	14	**15**	16	17	18	19
20	**21**	**22**	23	24	25	26
27	28	**29**	30	31		

- 1   INFUSION: Fourteenth Herceptin
- 1   VISIT: Pre Surgical Evaluation
- 7   CELEBRATE: My 46th Birthday!
- 8   VISIT: Appointment with Dr. Joseph
- 11   SURGERY: Remove Expanders & Insert Breast Implants
- 15   VISIT: Post-Op Appointment with Dr. Kaufman
- 21   INFUSION: Fifteenth Herceptin
- 21   VISIT: Appointment with Dr. Hergenroeder
- 22   VISIT: Appointment with Dr. Kaufman
- 22   PROCEDURE: Chest Drains Removed
- 29   VISIT: Appointment with Dr. Kaufman

JUNE 2018

12 INFUSION: Sixteenth Herceptin

26 VISIT: Appointment with Dr. Kaufman

SUN	MON	TUE	WED	THU	FRI	SAT
					1	2
3	4	5	6	7	8	9
10	11	12	13	14	15	16
17	18	19	20	21	22	23
24	25	26	27	28	29	30

JULY 2018

3 INFUSION: Seventeenth Herceptin

24 INFUSION: Eighteenth Herceptin

SUN	MON	TUE	WED	THU	FRI	SAT
1	2	3	4	5	6	7
8	9	10	11	12	13	14
15	16	17	18	19	20	21
22	23	24	25	26	27	28
29	30	31				

AUGUST 2018

14 VISIT: Appointment with Dr. Kaufman

17 VISIT: Appointment with Dr. Hergenroeder

17 PROCEDURE: Blood Work

SUN	MON	TUE	WED	THU	FRI	SAT
			1	2	3	4
5	6	7	8	9	10	11
12	13	14	15	16	17	18
19	20	21	22	23	24	25
26	27	28	29	30	31	

SEPTEMBER 2018

27 VISIT: Appointment with Dermatologist

SUN	MON	TUE	WED	THU	FRI	SAT
						1
2	3	4	5	6	7	8
9	10	11	12	13	14	15
16	17	18	19	20	21	22
23	24	25	26	**27**	28	29
30						

OCTOBER 2018

9 PROCEDURE: ECHOCardiogram
19 PROCEDURE: Bloodwork
22 VISIT: Appointment with Dr. Hergenroeder

SUN	MON	TUE	WED	THU	FRI	SAT
	1	2	3	4	5	6
7	8	**9**	10	11	12	13
14	15	16	17	18	**19**	20
21	**22**	23	24	25	26	27
28	29	30	31			

NOVEMBER 2018

6 VISIT: Appointment with Dr. Joseph
13 VISIT: Appointment with Dr. Kaufman

SUN	MON	TUE	WED	THU	FRI	SAT
				1	2	3
4	5	**6**	7	8	9	10
11	12	**13**	14	15	16	17
18	19	20	21	22	23	24
25	26	27	28	29	30	

DECEMBER 2018

SUN	MON	TUE	WED	THU	FRI	SAT
						1
2	3	4	5	6	7	8
9	10	11	12	13	14	15
16	17	18	19	20	21	22
23	24	25	26	27	28	29
30	31					

NOT a misprint.
No appointments this month!

JANUARY 2019

SUN	MON	TUE	WED	THU	FRI	SAT
		1	2	3	4	5
6	7	8	9	10	11	12
13	14	15	16	17	18	19
20	21	22	23	24	25	26
27	28	29	30	31		

11 VISIT: Appointment with Dermatologist
15 VISIT: Appointment with Dr. Resnick

FEBRUARY 2019

SUN	MON	TUE	WED	THU	FRI	SAT
					1	2
3	4	5	6	7	8	9
10	11	12	13	14	15	16
17	18	19	20	21	22	23
24	25	26	27	28		

5 VISIT: Appointment with Dr. Kaufman

NOT a misprint.
No appointments this month!

MARCH 2019

SUN	MON	TUE	WED	THU	FRI	SAT
					1	2
3	4	5	6	7	8	9
10	11	12	13	14	15	16
17	18	19	20	21	22	23
24	25	26	27	28	29	30
31						

NOT a misprint.
No appointments this month!

APRIL 2019

SUN	MON	TUE	WED	THU	FRI	SAT
	1	2	3	4	5	6
7	8	9	10	11	12	13
14	15	16	17	18	19	20
21	22	23	24	25	26	27
28	29	30				

7 CELEBRATE: My 47th Birthday!
7 VISIT: Appointment with Dr. Kaufman
20 VISIT: Appointment with Dr. Tamaskar
20 PROCEDURE: Blood Draw

MAY 2019

SUN	MON	TUE	WED	THU	FRI	SAT
			1	2	3	4
5	6	7	8	9	10	11
12	13	14	15	16	17	18
19	20	21	22	23	24	25
26	27	28	29	30	31	

19 PROCEDURE: Blood Draw

JUNE 2019

SUN	MON	TUE	WED	THU	FRI	SAT
						1
2	3	4	5	6	7	8
9	10	11	12	13	14	15
16	17	18	**19**	20	21	22
23	24	25	26	27	28	29
30						

15 INFUSION: Second Zometa
16 PROCEDURE: Chest Port Removal

JULY 2019

SUN	MON	TUE	WED	THU	FRI	SAT
	1	2	3	4	5	6
7	8	9	10	11	12	13
14	**15**	**16**	17	18	19	20
21	22	23	24	25	26	27
28	29	30	31			